THE NEPHILIM
BARBELL PROGRAM

By John Thacker, Jr.

Contents

Introduction

The Nephilim were on the earth in those days....
they were the heroes of old, men of renown.
- Genesis 6:4

Why Nephilim? Of all the mascots to represent my brand of strength training, why would I pick mythical antediluvian giants? Because they were men of renown. Because all these years later, we still remember them for moving heavy rocks around into impressive monuments to their tenacity and brute strength. The Nephilim Barbell Program is a strength training program designed for men of renown, and fearsome stone-wielding giants are the perfect metaphor for what we are becoming. Life is too short not to.

A dolmen in Jordan. The Nephilim made their name by moving heavy shit. So can you.

But life is also complicated, and when I began my strength building journey a few years ago, I quickly came to an important realization. The vast majority of real strength training programs are written by – and for – those who lift weights for a living. This makes a significant difference in terms of the resources one is able to dedicate to strength training – especially time. For the most part, the programs that *aren't* written by professional strength athletes are steaming piles of crap designed to do little more than perpetuate the "fitness" scam that is creating a generation of humans who can do a whole lot of kipping pull-ups but couldn't climb out of a burning building to save their own life.

The Nephilim Barbell Program is designed for normal humans who have to balance a real job and real life with the goal of becoming freakishly strong. As such, the Nephilim Barbell Program probably differs significantly from much of what you have read on the internet about getting strong. In the following paragraphs, I outline some of the differences in approach and philosophy that you can expect to find in this program.

Recovery

Most real strength programs were written by people who take steroids. Like it or not, it is a fact. There are some "clean" or "natty" (natural) powerlifters and strength trainers out there, but they are not only a minority in the sport, they are a minority in media. Steroids, or more precisely PEDs (Performance Enhancing Drugs) affect strength, but more importantly, how much work a person can do and recover from, as well as the speed of recovery. The Nephilim Barbell Program does not judge those who choose to use PEDs, but I have never used PEDs in any form, and this program is written for normal people who want to get freaking strong without sacrificing their health, their future, or their ability to get an erection after age 40. And that approach influences how the Nephilim Barbell Program is structured.

As well, most of the modern strength programs I read all seemed to be written by people who had hours to train every day, and eight hours of sleep to recover. As if. Some of us have real jobs. Some of us can't take sixteen meal breaks a day, nor spend an hour in an Epsom salt bath after using a foam roller for thirty minutes. Some of us are men of renown outside the weight-room, as well as inside it. All of this affects the effectiveness of any given strength training program design. The Nephilim Barbell Program is designed for people like me – working professionals who have to spend 50-60 hours in the office, have kids and a family, and feel damn lucky to get seven hours of sleep in a night.

Training Gear

Most strength programs out there assume access to advanced training gear - PEDs for sure, but also things like chains, bands, football bars, safety bars, and 300 lb. dumbbells. Not to mention constant access to a well-stocked refrigerator. If you have access to those things, great. If not, congratulations; you're normal. The Nephilim Barbell Program is built around moving lots of heavy stuff that nearly everyone has access too. A concrete floor and barbell is all you need to get started. Don't worry; we'll cover training gear and nutrition and all the rest, but you don't need to join a $150 per month strongman gym to get insanely strong with the Nephilim Barbell Program. In fact, you don't have to join a gym at all, but we'll cover that as well just to take some of the guesswork out.

Nutrition

Most strength training programs are designed around eating. A lot. In fact, powerlifters often brag that they eat whatever food they can get their hands on, and low-flying birds and small children when they can't. This is not strictly true, but it is a persistent myth. The Nephilim Barbell Program, on the other hand, will outline the principles required to get freakishly strong while living a normal balanced life and eating a normal, balanced diet (ok, not normal, but it should be). We will cover macros, supplements, and the rest, but believe it or not most people outside of Olympic athletes can get all they need at the grocery store. That's where I get my nutrition, and I can deadlift your subcompact.

My Own Story

For those of you who are wondering, my three lift total is just over 1500 lbs. That is generally the magic line that separates truly world-class strength athletes from the rest of the pack. I accomplished this over *years* of hard work inside and outside of the gym. I developed the Nephilim Barbell Program while living real life. It took a few years of trial and error, but once I found my groove, my strength gains increased at a geometric rate. I believe this program can work for you as well, and I designed it specifically for people like me – people who have a real life to live, a real family to raise, and yet still want to be brutally strong.

I started this program while married, and while working it I had two children, got my Masters degree, and tripled my income. I am active in my community, active in my fraternity, and volunteer with Kids Against Hunger every chance I get. I have a full life. I can also squat a quarter of a ton. Why not? Life is too short to leave anything on the table. I did all this without ever using any performance enhancing drugs. In fact, I've never used anything much more potent than creatine monohydrate, and even then I can only afford whatever off-brand they are selling at the grocery store. We'll cover supplements in more depth later, but the point is that I know how to make gains the old fashioned way, and I intend to help you do the same.

On the following pages I will cover the groundwork of lifting – the principles of lifting, the principles of this program, the basics of the core strength lifts, and the lifting program itself. We will then look at recovery, including sleep and nutrition. Remember, this program is not complete without all three components – stress (lifting), recovery, and nutrition. You may be tempted to skip this part of the book if you are an experienced lifter and get straight to the workout, but I recommend you look through it. You might learn a thing or two, and understanding the principles of the Nephilim Barbell Program will allow you to apply the program more effectively.

How Muscles Work

The science of strength training has a long history. Much like physics, strength training knowledge has always been pursued in two avenues – the theoretical side and the practical side. The theoretical side involves controlled experiments, chemistry, endocrinology, and other good science. The practical side involves going outside and moving heavy shit around. This is where "bro science" comes from – people who actually move stuff around are often strongly opinionated about what works, and sometimes resentful when theory seems to contradict their practice. I built my method from science, through years of applying theory in the gym. As such, this program draws on both streams. While you may just want to go out and get big and strong, it doesn't hurt to understand the science behind strength. Being ignorant, on the other hand, never helped anyone.

The default setting for the human body (or any living organism) is called *homeostasis*. This term, coined by Walter Cannon, captures how the body tends to stay within normal operating parameters. Hans Seyle expanded on this idea, by experimenting on how organisms (in this case, lab rats) responded to chemical stimuli. He mapped his results into three phases, which he collectively referred to as General Adaptation Syndrome. General Adaptation Syndrome, or GAS, comprises alarm, resistance, and exhaustion. The alarm stage is triggered when an organism is introduced to stress. This stage floods the body with hormones like adrenaline, and is similar to the "fight or flight" response. This is a short term response, and if the stress continues, the organism will enter the resistance phase; this phase sees the organism attempt to adapt to the stress. The final phase is exhaustion – if the stress continues past the organism's ability to resist, cell death will begin to occur.

If you are more intelligent than your average orangutan, then you already see where I am going with this science – building strength requires a person to tax their body with enough stress to get past the alarm stage, but not so much that they enter the exhaustion stage. In the former case, the body won't adapt and grow bigger or stronger; in the latter case, the body *still* won't grow bigger or stronger – it will break down and cause injury and disease (Rhabdomyolysis is a real overtraining disease, not a myth; that being said, I have yet to see anyone with the pain threshold to actually trigger this disease. Every single case I have ever seen involved someone using PEDs, and was the result of over-stimulating the steroid receptors. Don't use self-diagnosis of rhabdomyolysis or any other disease as an excuse not to train).

That's the 40,000 foot view. However, how the human body – and even just musculature in itself – works is significantly more complex. Your muscles consist of three different types of fibers. Slow oxidative fibers (Type I) are recruited first in muscular activity, fatigue slowly, and use aerobic glycolysis to produce adenosine triphosphate. These muscles contract slowly

SKELETAL MUSCLE

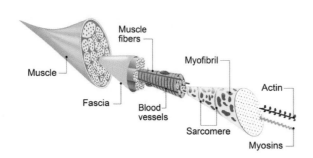

and are good for endurance exercise like running marathons (Yes, there are people who do this. No, I don't know why either). Fast oxidative fibers (Type IIa) are recruited second in muscular activity, fatigue a bit more rapidly than Type I, and contract much more quickly. These muscles work well for exercise that requires both aerobic and anaerobic endurance.

Fast glycolytic fibers (Type IIb) are the ninjas of the muscle fiber world. These muscles are recruited last in exercise, and do not use oxygen for fuel (in other words, they rely entirely on sugar to activate...keep that in mind for when we go over nutrition later). These muscles fatigue very quickly, but are very explosive. They are best suited for exercise like strength training. You may hear that humans actually have five types of muscle fibers, but that is getting into the semantic weeds at that point. These three types of fibers are all you need to know about muscle recruitment for your training purposes.

When subjected to stress, muscles adapt. There are two types of adaptation most commonly referenced in the world of barbell training – hypertrophy and hyperplasia. The former is often referred to in bro-science as "gettin' swole". The muscle fibers get larger. In reality, "getting swole" is often just pumping the muscles full of blood and water – this is not the same thing as hypertrophy. With hypertrophy, the individual muscle fibers are bigger during homeostasis – no need to "get a pump" or take fancy supplements to engorge the muscles. Hyperplasia, on the other hand, refers to actually adding new muscle fibers. Ok, it is more complex than that, and is most often associated with disease – in fact, an enlarged prostate is the result of hyperplasia.

Hyperplasia is a normal response of healthy cells under some conditions, and is controlled through normal regulatory mechanisms. Cell division or creation that is *not* subject to normal regulation is called neoplasia, and is a precursor to tumor growth. One normal regulatory mechanism that causes hyperplasia is Human Growth Hormone, or HGH. This is one of the more common PEDs used in the strength training world. However, a common theory is that hyperplasia can be stimulated through specific strength programming[1]. While this has yet to be proven with the rigor that constitutes true science, the experimental side has been going at it for a while, and bro-science agrees that hyperplasia is, in fact, possible. Theoretical science is getting closer to confirming this. In the 1980s, researchers found that powerlifters had the largest muscle fibers (hypertrophy), while bodybuilders had smaller fibers (in fact, they found that the fibers were the same size as in non-bodybuilders) – but bodybuilders had a lot more of them (hyperplasia). Unfortunately, this result has been called into question simply due to the fact that bodybuilders at the time were using all kinds of PEDs. This is not to say that powerlifters weren't, but only that we don't know if hyperplasia requires artificial stimulation or might be possible simply through training routine.

The bottom line is that science can't yet demonstrate that hyperplasia can be stimulated in humans through training methodology, but dudes that actually lift weights have been using specific training methods to increase hyperplasia for a couple of decades now[2]. Fred Koch's Periodization program is a classic example. The Nephilim Barbell Program uses methods intended to target both hypertrophy and hyperplasia. Bigger muscle fibers *and* more muscle fibers is the goal of this program. Because more and bigger means stronger.

Unfortunately, all this talk about muscles and myofibril hypertrophy and other gym-nerd topics, while fun, distract from the main point – the human body is not a muscle fiber, or even a collection of muscle fibers. The human body is a collection of *systems.* This is why bodybuilders look like Greek Gods, but can't move the kind of heavy weight that powerlifters can – and why powerlifters can perform insane feats of strength with a barbell, but can't use that strength in meaningful ways like a strongman pulling a jet with a rope. The strongman and powerlifter train *systems*, while the bodybuilder trains muscles. As well, the strongman trains for functional strength, while the powerlifter trains to move a barbell in three specific movements. The Nephilim Barbell Program takes the systems approach to strength development – the body is an integrated whole, and the Nephilim Barbell Program integrates training, recovery, and nutrition in holistic ways to allow you to become freakishly strong without sacrificing a "normal" life.

---

[1] Kisner, Carolyn; Colby, Lynn Allen (2012-10-08). Therapeutic Exercise: Foundations and Techniques. F.A. Davis. ISBN 9780803638976.

[2] MacDougal, J. 1992. Hypertrophy or hyperplasia. Strength and Power in Sport, ed. P. Komi, 230-38. London: Blackwell Scientific Publishing.
Sjostrom, M. et al. 1991. Evidence of fiber hyperplasia in human skeletal muscles from healthy young men? European Journal of Applied Physiology 62:310-4.
Umnova, M., and T. Seene. 1991. The effect of increased functional load on the activation of satellite cells in the skeletal muscles of adult rats. International Journal of Sports Medicine 12:501-4.

Weight Lifting Basics

This is not a book about how to lift. If you are a novice – or even just someone who hasn't spent the proper time thinking about what strength training is – go pick up Mark Rippetoe's *Starting Strength: Basic Barbell Training*[3]. This is the Bible of barbell training, and I'm not going to waste everyone's time rehashing what he says in that book. Besides, he is smarter and more knowledgeable than I am, especially in physiology, so just go read his book. Having said that, I will cover some brief basics to make sure we are on the same page. If you don't understand anything in this section, or have questions *stop the program*. You need to spend some time educating yourself before proceeding.

Gear

Weightlifting gear falls into four main categories: clothing, bracing, grip, and PEDs. Gear is one of the more discussed topics in the sport (surprisingly), and while I won't shove a dissertation down your throat, it is important to understand the basics outlined below.

Clothing

Clothing may not sound important to a beginner, but it is extremely important. Not to be crass, but start with your underpants. You need panties that let you do compound movements without bunching

Feel free to wear a shirt while working out.

up or giving you a wedgie. No boxers! The best underwear you can wear is going to be a pair of athletic compression shorts like those from Under Armor or Nike (I own both). You do *not* want a tight pair that truly compresses your upper thigh (bicycle shorts are like this). Also, while you are putting on your panties, go ahead and use some baby powder on the old crack. You will be sweating, and you don't want an itchy pool of gravy distracting you from lifting. Moving on to the pants, you want something tight enough to not get caught while you are lifting, but obviously loose enough to allow the kinds of compound movements necessary to lift. It may look cool to

---

[3] Mark Rippetoe, *Starting Strength: Basic Barbell Training* (Wichita Falls, Tex.: The Asgard Company, 2013).

lift in combat boots and tattered jeans with a wife-beater, but it's stupid as hell. To be honest, women have a bit of an advantage here, since it has become acceptable for them to wear "yoga pants" (fancy name for skin-tight drawers) while working out. These provide plenty of mobility while also being tight enough that you don't have to worry about accidentally snagging them on your knuckles while deadlifting. For my part, I wear sweatpants. Yeah, I'm that guy.

Your shirt needs to be snug, but not tight. You don't want to chafe (may sound funny, but especially as you get larger, you will find that cotton t-shirts often chafe around the armpits and shoulders while doing upper body work), but a loose shirt is dangerous. As well, if you work with a spotter or trainer, a more snug shirt allows the spotter to assess your form by how the wrinkles form. This is one area where women do not have an advantage – those tight tanks that are all the rage don't have enough slack to help with form evaluation. That being said, tight is generally better than loose. The last thing you want to do is catch your thumb in your shirt while performing 150 pound Kroc Rows.

Finally, but most importantly, your clothing includes your shoes. There is all kind of information out there about this, but I will make it really simple for you. You want little to no sole, and never *ever* wear running shoes to lift weights. The reason for this is simple. As you progress in strength you will begin using weights that dramatically exceed the capability of most sneakers. The sole will literally slide out from under your feet. I wear Chuck Taylors by Converse. These are popular with powerlifters because they are cheap and they work (and let's face it, they have a built in "screw the world" attitude). There are purpose built weight-lifting shoes, and they are mostly good as well. These shoes usually come with a small wedge heal, which can be hugely helpful if you have limited mobility. Imagine the form of a squat. At the bottom, that little half inch heel is one half inch less that your Achilles' tendon has to stretch. However, I have never, ever felt stable while wearing these kinds of shoes. I would avoid "cross-fit" shoes altogether. They are more expensive than lifting shoes, generally less well constructed, and are basically a marketing gimmick. Also, you may have noticed some powerlifters lifting in their socks – or you may have practiced this yourself. Chances are, your gym doesn't allow this for sanitary reasons, but if it does, I would caution you to avoid the habit if possible. The main reason is that most gym floors can be pretty damn slippery if you start sweating through your socks. The other is that it is only a matter of time before you drop a weight or roll a barbell over your foot. Without shoes, this could actually cause you an injury. That being said, if you are dirt poor like I was when I started, just put your damn three year old running shoes in the corner and lift in your socks.

Bracing

There are several bracing products out there. The most basic is the lifting belt. The lifting belt should absolutely be a part of your gym bag. There are a few different types of lifting belt, but they all serve the same purpose – that purpose is to provide a brace for your abs to push against while  lifting insanely heavy weights. The first style is the Olympic lifting belt. Because the Olympic lifts are more dynamic, this belt is narrower. That's ok, but you probably want something a bit wider. 3" is probably good. The second type is the Velcro synthetic belt. This kind of belt lacks the rigidity of a leather belt, and is often marketed to females. They seem to work ok, but I personally won't use a belt that is secured with Velcro. The third type is the "bodybuilding" belt that has a pad in back that is wider than the belt in front. I do not understand this design, since it contradicts the purpose of the lifting belt – don't get this kind. The last kind is the powerlifting belt. This is a single width belt, generally 3" wide, and usually made of cowhide between 8-10mm. There are two main clasping systems – the old fashioned belt buckle, and the modern quick release clasp. The quick release clasp is much easier to get on and off. Having said that, I find the clasp to be very difficult to work with if I'm trying to do dynamic lifts like a clean and jerk, or any barbell movement where the bar comes above my waist. It catches on the clasp. I use an old fashioned 3" powerlifting belt made of 10mm steer-hide with a two-prong buckle. You absolutely must have a belt in your gym bag, but don't over use it. I use mine on squats and deadlifts only, and only on my heaviest sets. I will occasionally use a belt for Military Press, but the purpose is to help your core muscles, not keep them from growing on their own. Below is a list of a few other types of bracing gear:

Wrist wraps: these are supposed to support your wrists during heavy pushing motions. While your wrist does include many tiny bones, I have never understood or had to use wrist wraps. I do wear them loosely while doing Kroc Rows, but this is only because the weights at the gym where I work out sometimes rotate and bang into my wrist. The wraps are just to prevent bruising. If you start benching north of 400, you can wear whatever you damn well please on your wrists.

Knee wraps: I have never used knee wraps, so I may not be the guy to talk to about these. I would say that unless your doctor says to wear them, then don't. They do affect your ability to get stronger, and they change the dynamic of lower body lifts. If you are having knee pain then you are probably doing cardio wrong. You may also be doing your lifting wrong, lifting too heavy, not warming up properly, or lifting with incorrect form. You may also have a disease like degenerative tissue disease, in which case wraps won't help you anyway. What you don't want to do is grow your legs stronger without growing your knees stronger. You can't build Stonehenge with shit knees.

Gimmicks: I just lumped all the other bracing tools into the category of gimmicks. Lifting suits or shirts are just gimmicks. Sure, there is the gorilla who benches 500 in a three-ply shirt, but who wants to be that guy who can't lift shit without a special shirt? Furthermore, the shirt changes the way you lift. No shortcuts, and no gimmicky crap.

Grip

The most important gear for grip is chalk. This doesn't increase your grip per se, but it does keep that shiny metal bar from sliding around in your greasy sweat. It is a safety tool, so use it. If your gym doesn't allow it, use it anyway. If they kick you out tell them that that you can't support a gym that cares more about vacuuming than about your safety. Safety first.

Another common grip tool is the lifting strap. Try not to use these. You want to actually get strong, and that means your grip strength needs to increase. Straps will inhibit that. However, I do use straps on occasion under specific conditions. Your back is a much, much larger group of muscles than your forearm, and sometimes your grip will tire before your back has received a proper workout. In these instances, I will use straps for dumbbell rows, powershrugs, etc. Basically, if I'm doing a lot of reps I will use straps when my grip starts to tire. I never *ever* use straps for deadlifts. Last but not least is the venerable lifting glove. Lose 'em.

If your gym cares more about vacuuming up chalk than they do about your safety, it is time to find a new gym.

PEDs

Performance enhancing drugs are ubiquitous in the strength training world. In fact, they are ubiquitous in your local YMCA. Opinions on PEDs and their uses are mixed, and generally strong. While the Nephilim Barbell Program does not condemn the use of steroids or other PEDs, it is specifically designed for those 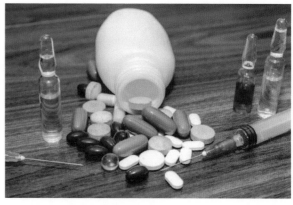 who do not use steroids. There are several reasons for this, but the bottom line is that unless you are trying to be a world class athlete, there really is no need to use steroids. The proper lifting, recovery, and nutrition structure can get you strong as a bear without the cost and risk of using steroids. If, however, you do choose to use PEDs, please talk to your doctor about it and make sure that you are using quality product and are on an intelligent plan. Do not risk your health and safety over something as silly as lifting weights.

Miscellaneous

Ok, so I lied; there are five categories of gear. The last category of gear is miscellaneous. A common example might be a belt designed to let you chain weight around your waist to do weighted dips. Or bands (you don't need bands). Or chains (really? I mean they look cool in a Conan sort of way, but you couldn't think of a *quieter* way to increase resistance?). Bottom line is that you don't need any of this crap to run the Nephilim Barbell Program. Once you can bench over 300 pounds, then you have earned the right to start messing around with crap. Chance are, by the time you get there you won't need to[4].

---

[4] To be fair, some of these items become important tools for increasing strength once a person exceeds 90% of their potential. However, we are talking about people who bench press over 400 pounds. In my experience most intermediate lifters use junk like bands and chains as an excuse not to keep driving their gains through hard work and pain.

The Big Four

The Nephilim Barbell Program is designed around the so-called "big four" of barbell training exercises. These are the Bench Press, Overhead Press, Squat, and Deadlift. There are many other lifts in the program, and we will illustrate some of these as we go, but for now it is *very* important to understand these four main lifts.

Some general advice before we dive in: First, go ahead and look some of these movements up on the internet. There are a lot of good videos of people who know what they are doing. There is also a lot of crap from doofuses who don't know squat and are trying to sell ignorance to desperate shlubs. Don't be a desperate shlub. Second, practice these lifts. Practice your form. You might be able to get away with sloppy form when you are squatting 225, but when you are squatting 545 that same poor form will crush your legs like a stale corn dog at the county fair. Use light weight while practicing – like a barbell if you are strong enough, or even a broom stick or pipe if you aren't. Seriously. You have to think long term here. If you really want to deadlift a quarter ton or more, you have to lift for many years and be relatively injury free. Practice your form. Third, stay athletic. The Nephilim Barbell Program includes built in work to keep you athletic, but at the end of the day, the best way to stay limber and athletic is to participate in some kind of sport. It is also the best way to get injured. I haven't checked the stats recently, but the last time I did, the number one cause of sports related injuries was basketball. Don't play basketball. You don't need a torn MCL or abraded patellar meniscus when you're trying to lift heavy stuff. Again, think long-term. I won't tell you not to play Ultimate Frisbee on the weekends, but if you're Katy Competition out there and end up with a sprained wrist don't say I didn't warn you. Fourth, if you do sustain an injury, *see a doctor, stupid*. No excuses. You have to get better to get better. I suppose that this is as a good a place as any to let you know that I am not a sports physiologist, and everything I've written in this book is for your learning enjoyment. Do not begin this or any program without consulting your physician first. Seriously. You don't want to be halfway through a 300 plus pound bench press to find out you have an aortic aneurism. Use your brain, genius. I don't personally engage in sports, other than the occasional pick-up soccer match (yes, I look as funny as that sounds). Instead, I use the elliptical machine to perform HIIT, as outlined later in the program. I highly recommend frequent HIIT sessions to stay in shape.

Bench Press

The bench press is the king of bro strength. If some idiot in the gym asks you, "How much do you lift?" They are probably talking about bench press. That being said, the bench is one of the more useless exercises. In fact, when you think about functional strength, pushing is almost always combined with a lift motion, and generally is part of a larger full-body exercise. For example, pushing is used in the tire flip for strong man competitions. But this action also involves squatting, lifting, etc. So don't take the bench too seriously or make it the focus of your life like some insecure idiot. The bench is also the most technically complex lift of the "big four". Surprised? Don't be. It is the most isolated of the four, and takes a significant amount of practice to get the form right.

This sketch demonstrates proper bench press form. Notice the feet flat on the floor, the leg drive with arched back, the proper position of the bar over the sternum, the narrower grip, and the elbow tuck.

"Proper" form will be, at least in part, determined by your physiology. Again, if you haven't read Mark Rippetoe's "Starting Strength", go out and buy it right now. The mechanics and form of lifting are beyond the scope of this book. Having said that, here are some basics to keep in mind while benching. First, keep your butt in contact with the bench, and learn to use leg drive. Second, fill your lungs with air before every rep. Third, squeeze your scapulae (shoulder blades) together and keep your shoulders down. Fourth, use a narrower grip, and keep your elbows tucked in. I actually use my triceps and lats to "catch" the weight at the bottom. It will take some bulking before you can do this, but just remember to tuck your elbows slightly as you come down. Fifth, keep tension in the press all the way to the bottom. Do *not* let the weight fall the last two inches (most common error I see in benching). Do *not* bounce the weight off your chest. But do make sure that you always touch your chest. Hold it for one half second, then press up. This is how powerlifters do it, and they are stronger than you. Copy them. Fifth, do *not* use a false grip (thumb under the bar going the same direction as your other fingers). I have seen way too many injuries when the weight slips out.

Squat

The squat is the king of strength exercises. The squat activates the entire body, and strengthens the core like nobody's business. To maximize your strength gains consider the following: First, get your form right.

Low bar position squat with properly tight upper back.

Then practice it with no weight (like, a broomstick – for real). Do this until you understand not only the proper groove, but what happens when you move out of your proper groove. Second, squat to proper depth. "Ass to grass" is probably too low; believe it or not, going too low can negatively affect your form. However, when you are squatting to proper depth it will probably feel like ass to grass. Check your ego at the door, Napoleon. If you can't squat to depth with the proper form at your current workout weights, drop the weight and learn how to do it right. No cheating, and no excuses. Third, learn to properly tighten your upper back. Fourth, if you have long arms like I do, then you run the risk of supporting the bar with your wrists. Position your hands so that they are behind and over the bar, so that your back takes the weight, and not your wrists. Fifth, always use the low-back position. Always.

Overhead Press

The overhead press is the single greatest pressing motion for building mass and functional strength. If you can only do one strength building exercise for the upper body, it should be this one. In the "old days", the single greatest test of masculine strength was how much could be cleaned and pressed overhead. In fact, the exercise was so revered that the AAU put strict rules around how it could be performed. The weight had to touch the torso, pause, and then be pressed overhead in a controlled manner, with no kind of leg drive (i.e., push press) or torso involvement. And it had to be cleaned from the floor. Today, the overhead press has fallen into disuse among many. That's a pity, because there is a direct correlation between how much a person can overhead press and their general bad-assitude.

Having said all that, the overhead press is less dangerous than the bench press (if you drop the weight, you can avoid it crushing you more easily), but still requires some technical precision to avoid injury. Well fuck, I better get over saying that. All the big four require technical precision to avoid injury. That being said, poor form on a squat or deadlift will give you fair warning long before you injure yourself. The same can not be said of the overhead press. There are two common injuries associated with the overhead press. The first is the dreaded and mysterious "shoulder impingement". There are all kinds of misunderstanding around this symptom (impingement syndrome is not a diagnosis; it is symptom). The easiest way to understand this syndrome is to imagine your shoulder (and back) muscles passing through a ring of bone. As the bones move, they can pinch the muscles. This is pretty close to accurate for our purposes. The supraspinatus muscle passes under the acromial arch, which is formed by the confluence of the acromion, corocroid process, and scapula. The easiest way to avoid this injury is to keep the elbows pointed *forward* while lifting. Try an experiment without any weight – put your hands in the barbell pressing position but without any weight. Point your elbows forward. Now rotate your elbows outward. You can actually feel your shoulders tighten up; as your scapula

Karen intentionally demonstrates improper form. Notice the distally rotated scapula and extreme wrist angle.

rotates, the subacromial arch constricts. The other common injury is wrist pain. This one is an easy fix and applies to all other pressing motions, including even holding the barbell during a squat. The bar should not sit "deep" in the grip, but rather across the meaty part of the lower palm, and the bar should remain directly above the wrist throughout the duration of the exercise.

Some overhead press tips: Take this exercise seriously. Always perform it standing. While variations like the push press can be essential to developing functional strength or training for strongman, try not to replace this lift in your arsenal. Keep your core tight. Avoid arching your back, especially at the top. This is a sign of a tight upper back. It is very common for the teres minor and/or infraspinatus to shorten after resistance exercise; this is why mobility work is important. If your upper back gets tight, the reduced range of motion (ROM) will cause

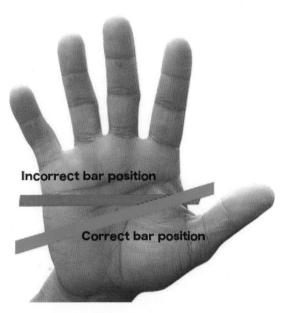

the lifter to hyper extend the lumbar vertebrae in order to lock out at top. This is dangerous and stupid. Don't be dangerous and stupid.

Deadlift

The deadlift is a simple test that answers the question "how much can you pick up off the ground?" It is personally my favorite lift, except when I'm doing squats. I like squats a lot. The biggest error I see in the deadlift is people exaggerating the arch in their lower back before pulling. This is generally the result of a misapplied zeal for proper form. Ironically, so doing actually increases the risk of injury. The lower back needs to be straight, and

for those with thick muscles or some body fat, you won't even see an arch. Keep your back tight and don't overemphasize the spinal curvature. On the other hand, brand new lifters often let their lower back slide into a sloppy curve that roughly imitates a constipated Labrador retriever trying to take a dump. These are two sides to the same injury coin.

The most common amateur mistake in mechanics is trying to jerk the bar off the floor. No. Keep your entire body tight like a coiled spring. If your shoulders move, the bar should move. Think of the link between your shoulders and the bar as a piece of tempered steel. There is no flex, no bounce, no whip. Pull with your back and legs. Any "pull" with your arms or upper body that occurs before the bar clears your knees will kill the motion anyway.

Last but not least, please don't hitch or otherwise compromise your lower back and your dignity. If you can lift over 500 lbs. it is acceptable to hitch *slightly* in order to lockout. But remember that you are not in competition in the gym. Better to miss a lift and live to fight another day than to prance around like a cat on a hot skillet just to claim a dubious PR increase.

This lifter demonstrates the alternative "sumo" setup. This is a more technically demanding setup that improves leverages. Not recommended for general mass building, and illegal in strong man competitions.

Choosing a Gym

To get big and strong, you need a gym with basic barbells and dumbbells. If you read through the program, you will find that the only other equipment you might want includes parallel bars for dips and a chin-up bar for chins and leg raises. You also want a gym that lets you grunt, use chalk, and do heavy, dangerous exercises. This will likely eliminate most of the tacky, trendy, "fitness" centers that make millions by convincing losers that it is ok to be a loser. Having said that, you don't need some expensive gym either. I actually work out at a national fitness chain. They let me use chalk, they have all the equipment I need, and it is about $20 a month, which is pretty cheap in my neck of the woods. There is an actual strongman gym near me, but it is damn near $150 a month dues. No thanks; I have kids to feed. The only thing I don't recommend is the home gym. Some very few (mostly very experienced) lifters can make this work, but the pressure of working out in front of others changes everything. As well, even a basic setup of *quality* benches and bars and plates (in other words, safe to use) will easily run north of $1,000 even if you get the equipment at yard sales. So my advice is look for a nice, old school gym with concrete floors, no air conditioning, and AC/DC at 90 decibels and give it a shot. $5 bottled water and a row of soccer moms wasting their life on elliptical machines are not essential to the Nephilim Barbell Program.

The Principles of the *Nephilim Barbell Program*

The Nephilim Barbell Program training is designed around four main principles. These principles were developed in the following manner: first, I read up on all the science and current knowledge on strength training. Second, I tried it out in the gym. Third I discovered what worked and what didn't – not just in the gym, but with my lifestyle. What was left, I distilled down into four principles as listed below. The program itself is prescriptive – you can literally just follow the steps and make gains – but it doesn't hurt to understand the underlying logic, especially as you mature in your lifting and make changes to the program to accommodate your evolving strength and lifestyle.

Principle 1: Proper Periodization

Periodization is like a pendulum. You can't lift your maximum amount of weight every week. Your body will break down, your gains will shrivel, and the only thing that will keep you from wasting your time in the gym is the significant injury you are likely to sustain. Periodization takes into account the way that human musculoskeletal grows. The Nephilim Barbell Program consists of an eight week cycle, followed by a one week deload. The first four weeks consist of volume training; the second four weeks consist of heavy training; the final week is a deload week.

The first four weeks comprise a classic "three by five" structure, with three working sets of five reps. Of course, there are multiple warmup sets leading up to the working set, so your total rep count will be higher than 15. This is a little bit lighter than many strength training programs, but there is a reason for that. The Nephilim Barbell Program incorporates a higher variety of pushing movements on chest day than just the bench. While you have to bench to get a stronger bench, other pressing motions will strengthen your core and ancillary muscles better. So chest day includes bench, narrow-grip press, and dips. In chapter nine we will talk about some alternatives for those with a compressed lifestyle or limited access to equipment. The point is that during the first four weeks we emphasize volume while progressively ramping up the effort.

Weeks five through eight emphasize heavy training. The volume drops, but the poundage increases significantly. These weeks also progress in weight, and the last week will come close to simulating a "peak" event like a competition. I say come close for two reasons. First, it is very difficult to truly peak every nine months, especially without taking any PEDs. Second, we don't go all out on the final week like we might in a competition.

The final week, a deload week, consists of letting your body rest. You will do the "big four" ONLY, and at light weight. This will be supplemented by stretching and mobility work. The point of a deload is to let your body rest, so these workouts are designed to keep your muscle memory in the groove and stimulate metabolism, not wear you out. During the deload week you will also calculate your new 1RM based on week eight.

This nine week cycle is designed to capitalize on your body's General Adaptation Syndrome. Just this method alone will increase the speed at which gains are made, while limiting the dreaded "plateau". However, there are other important methods that address how the actual weight lift is performed. These are covered in chapter seven, and are an important part of making your workouts as efficient as possible.

Principle 2: Proper Stimulation
The second foundational principle of the Nephilim Barbell Program is that of proper stimulation. You see, there are many different approaches to many different goals when moving heavy shit around the gym. One of my favorite athletes of all time is Brian Shaw of the USA. Brian Shaw is a World's Strongest Man competitor, and is just about the perfect picture of the "gentle giant". Of course, if you watch him compete you will begin to severely doubt the "gentle" part. He is probably as close to a modern Nephilim as you can get. Brian is a large man – 6' 8" tall (203 cm) and over 400 lbs (181 Kg) – and he throws 300 pound atlas stones around like basketballs. It should not be surprising to students of strength development that he grew up on a farm. Years of multiple joint movements spread out over the course of a work day is a natural precursor to being a strongman. Bodybuilders, on the other hand, emphasize isolation movements and time under tension. Powerlifters strive for maximal musculoskeletal load. Keep in mind that other athletes also use strength training to reach their own goals. This might include wind sprints, long distance running, or other exercises. The bottom line is that if you want to reach a specific goal, you have to follow a specific path. Willy-nilly training nets willy-nilly results. The specific goal of the Nephilim Barbell Program is to maximize efficient strength gains for people living a normal life. This specific goal includes the idea of staying healthy enough over time to continue to make gains, as well as the idea of having the resilience and adaptability to make gains when life throws curveballs at your training schedule. Which it will.

Remember chapter two on how muscles work? The training methods outlined in the Nephilim Barbell Program are designed to maximize hypertrophy and hyperplasia. Big and thick muscles mean strength gains. However, the types of exercises, the periodization and rest, the cardio, and the nutrition components are all designed to work together to maximize full body strength. So while the lifting program is designed to properly stimulate the muscles for maximal growth, the other components are essential to maximizing the efficiency of your gains.

Principle 3: Proper Rest

Rest is part of the strength building cycle – your muscles do not grow during your workout; they grow during rest. For this reason, proper rest is an essential principle of the Nephilim Barbell Program. There are actually three components of proper rest. The first is intra-workout rest. This is the amount of rest that you incorporate into your workout. If you remember from chapter two, different muscle fibers utilize different methods of producing energy. The Nephilim Barbell Program has specific recommended rest periods built around how muscle fibers work. During the Big Four, rest periods should be 90-180 seconds between sets. You will generally use 90 seconds between your warmup sets and lighter working sets, and the full 180 on your heavy sets. These periods are scientifically calculated based on how long it takes your body to restore cells. If you wait beyond 180 seconds, you will likely lose the "pump" and see a slight reduction in strength as well as blood pump that cushions heavy movements.

The second type of rest is the cyclical rest that allows your muscles to adapt to stress. The nine week cycle of the Nephilim Barbell Program is designed to do just that. As well, the important deload week gives your body time to adapt to the stress of placing near-maximal stress on the body.

The third type of rest is the general rest required to repair and replenish – sleep. This type of rest is also cyclical in nature, generally following the cycle of the sun. While we have created the technology to allow us to extend our work day past the natural cycle of the sun, our bodies have not yet evolved to match our technology. For this reason, it is generally healthiest and most effective to match your waking and sleeping cycles to the rhythm of the sun. Doctors recommend eight hours of sleep minimum, and many strength athletes recommend as much as ten hours of sleep to give your body time to grow. If your life is anything like mine, then that is a pipe dream. I do recommend eight hours of sleep a night – turn off the TV and lie in bed. It will take a full week or two, but your body will adapt and you will be able to go to sleep at 8 pm. Turn this into a ritual – follow the same pattern every night, at exactly the same time. Drink an herbal tea or other natural supplement to help you feel drowsy. Do NOT drink alcohol, as this will actually keep you from sleeping well. Use ear-plugs and eye-shades to help you sleep. It is worth it. Even utilizing these techniques I rarely get more than 7 hours of sleep a night. If you can, try supplementing your "gathered" nightly sleep with a noon nap. Prior to the commercialization of industry, this was a normal part of life, and it continues to this day in many nations, especially in equatorial climes. If you can squeeze an hour in, go for it. Many people actually feel more tired when they do this, but you have to enter REM sleep to really heal your body. A 15 minute power nap might do wonders for your concentration at work, but it will not help you repair your broke-down spinal erectors. Last but not least, don't sleep in. This tends to throw your sleep pattern off. When I "sleep in" I sleep for one extra hour. Anything more than that gets close to throwing my schedule off.

Principle 4: Proper Nutrition

It seems like everyone is talking nutrition these days. Macro this and micronutrient that – it's enough to make anyone binge out at Fat Burger just for spite. The Nephilim Barbell Program cuts through the bullshit and delivers the straight line on nutrition. There is an entire chapter dedicated to nutrition later on, but the principles of proper nutrition are simple. The first principle is to eat real whole foods. The second principle is to eat enough food. The third principle is to time your food properly. That's it. Real whole foods can be briefly summed up as eating food as it is found in nature. I make obvious exceptions – such as cooking your meat – but the farther from nature that your food is, the less nutritional value it contains. The only real exception I make to this "rule" is liquid nutrition: I do use powdered supplements mixed with water or milk in order to flood my body with nutrients as quickly as possible. Eating enough food is more difficult for many people than it sounds. Once you cut out all the junk it actually takes a lot of eating to get the proper calories. Just remember to eat like you get paid to. I'll bet all of us would have no problem preparing and eating enough healthy calories if someone were paying us to. Food timing, the third principle, involves getting the right amounts of the right nutrients in your body just before, during, and just after your workout. It also involves sleep, and what you eat right before bed. This is a complex enough topic that the details will be saved for the nutrition chapter.

The Core Components
Powerlifting

First, the Nephilim Barbell Program is designed around the core, tried-and-true, strength training barbell exercises. As we have already seen, these principles are also the basis of muscular hypertrophy. These four core exercises are the Bench Press, Squat, Overhead Press, and Deadlift. These are compound exercises that do more than build muscle – they make you strong. As far as weight training goes, these four lifts best simulate real-world strength. While it would be cool to design this program around strong-man exercises like atlas stones or the prowler, the bottom line is that most of America doesn't have access to equipment like that. I'm no exception. I built my strength at a $15/month hole-in-the-wall gym that had your basic barbells, some ratty dumbbells that barely went up to 80 lbs. (you know, the kind where the bolt that holds the weights on threatens to come out every third rep), and a set of machines that possibly pre-dated the original Nautilis equipment. Barbells just work.

Maximal Growth Stimulation

The Nephilim Barbell Program also makes use of maximal efficient growth stimulation. This is achieved by combining strength exercises with exercises specifically designed to stimulate hyperplasia while making sure your support muscles get the proper development. This is often referred to as "accessory work" which is a frankly silly phrase, since this work is just as important to your strength gains as the rest of the program. The Nephilim Barbell Program also includes a healthy amount of the right kind of cardio. Why? Think about it, genius. All those World's Strongest Men do plenty of cardio. Cardio is the basis for all athletic prowess. At some point, some ignorant know-it-all decided to tell people that too much cardio was bad for getting stronger or building muscle. That is total bullshit. There is not one single shred of scientific evidence to support that claim. It is an excuse from big fat people to not have to work as hard. If you want to be a strongman, or maximize your strength gains, or build a freaking pyramid out of giant stones, you have to be able to walk up to a squat rack without gassing out. And contrary to popular myth, cardio is actually essential for maximizing your growth and strength gains. So yes, the Nephilim Barbell Program includes cardio work. Deal with it.

To make your workouts as efficient as possible, I have distilled your physiological needs down to the most relevant exercises. Don't be that idiot doing 17 sets of barbell curls followed by 30 minutes of band pull aparts. The only thing you're doing in that case is taking up gym space and wasting my oxygen. You're also wasting your time. The Nephilim Barbell Program won't waste your time. I'll just end this segment by saying that the Nephilim Barbell Program is not for ego lifters. You want to look jacked and get scoped by the girls while lifting? Go copy some internet jackass. Don't forget to scream while maxing out on your barbell curls. The fact is, the Nephilim Barbell Program is designed by science to maximize your strength gains. And like it or not, science says that lifting heavy all the time doesn't make you stronger. You will get stronger on the Nephilim Barbell Program, and in a few months you'll be repping 405 on the deadlift and wondering how you got so strong. But if you want to show off, just go find another program now.

Consistent Small Gains
The Nephilim Barbell Program is also built around the core of consistent small gains. As much as we would all like to walk up to the power rack and smash our previous PR (Personal Record) in the squat by 50 lbs., the bottom line is that you are much more likely to bump it up a few pounds a week (keep in mind that the velocity of your gains is directly proportional to how advanced you are in your training). Now at some point you will "grow up" in your lifting, and begin to auto-regulate. This is a good thing, and when you reach this stage of development you will begin to shed some of the program in this book and begin tweaking it to your own needs. Fine. But until you get to that point you need to be making progress. Evidence and experience suggests that it is possible and preferable to make small gains consistently. It also gives you something to shoot for. I love trying to make

gains every week – it lights a fire under my ass and reminds me that I'm actually doing something with my time.

Proper Recovery

The Nephilim Barbell Program is also designed around is the core of proper recovery. Remember, *you don't grow in the gym*. Remember that paragraph a few pages ago about General Adaptation Syndrome? You have to stress your body into the resistance stage, but then give it time to adapt. The current research indicates that it takes 96 hours for a muscle group to fully recover. Because the Nephilim Barbell Program was designed to be used by regular, non-professional and un-sponsored humans, it is built around *realistic* recovery times and practices. For this reason, the Nephilim barbell Program only lifts weights four days a week – two days a week for upper body, and two days a week for lower body. If this doesn't fit your lifestyle, it will even work with only three workouts per week. The Nephilim Barbell Program also includes three days of High Intensity Interval Training (HIIT) three days per week. We will also discuss mobility (a hot new fad that refers to actually being slightly athletic – hint: the HIIT will help a lot with this), stretching, foam rolling, and all the other habits that may or may not help you get stronger. The Nephilim Barbell Program does all the planning for you so you don't have to waste your time experimenting like I did.

The Workout

The Nephilim Barbell Program is built around the following lifting schedule. This program is designed so that you can just follow it and grow big. No thinking required. But most of the seriously strong people I know are actually pretty deep thinkers, at least when it comes to strength training, so I wanted to go over the design principles of the big lifts. The big lifts are about increasing your ability to do work, but to specifically engineer that capacity increase into lifting more weight. For that reason, calculating your one repetition max, or "1RM" is essential. This is the benchmark against which your gains will be measured. And since you will be growing, your 1RM will change over time. Now this is where it gets weird. I have read all kinds of literature on calculating your 1RM, and then calculating your "training 1RM", and then all kinds of math hocus pocus. Let me break down the idea of "max" to you.

The only "real" max is the maximum amount of weight you have moved. If you compete, then your "real" max is the maximum amount of weight you have lifted in competition. Period. For every other purpose, "max" is an arbitrary and theoretical benchmark that allows you to peg your progress. I remember one "bro" using a calculator to calculate my "1RM" from a set of reps. Then he told me to take a percentage of that to use as my "training max". I remember looking at him like he was a particularly enlightened cabbage and asking why his calculator couldn't just figure that out from the get-go. Bottom line, this program just refers to your "1RM", and that term is a reference to your *calculated* max. What you are actually capable of lifting, or what you actually do lift may or may not be different.

While 1RM may be an arbitrary calculation against which to peg progress, it is important that everyone be using the *same* arbitrary calculation in order for this (or any) program to work. The calculations in this book are based on the most common method of calculating the 1RM, also known as the Epley method. This formula is as follows:

$$1RM = ((Number\ of\ Reps/30)+1) * weight\ used$$

Your first task will be to calculate your 1RM in the gym. Use enough weight that you can't quite hit ten reps. You want all your reps to be clean, though. Use the right form, and lock them out. Next, plug the weight you used and the reps you hit into the equation above. For example, if you got six reps on the bench press at 225 lbs., then your 1RM calculation would be $((6/30)+1)*225 = 1.2*225 = 270$. You will then use 270 as your 1RM for bench press calculations in the program to follow.

You will notice that the last set of the Big Four is a reduced weight set to "rep max". "Rep max" refers to the maximum number of reps you can perform at that weight after all the other work you've already done with your muscles. It is very important that this set be done with attention and with careful form. Do NOT perform "to failure". The program says *rep* max – that means you actually have to rep the weight. As a side note, I have performed the Nephilim Barbell Program for years with no spotter. The truth is, a spotter is supposed to watch you lift and coach your form – not help you lift the weight. For the big four, a spotter is unlikely to be able to help you avoid injury if you lift past your reasonable moment threshold. The only exception is the bench press; however, your spotter will naturally pull the weight over your shoulders if he or she has to assist, which will put much more strain on your shoulders and could result in injury as you progress to heavier weights. All that to say that "rep max" means the maximum number of clean reps that you can perform yourself, not some half-assed limited ROM wasted motion accompanied by a spotter taking half the workload off you anyway.

You will notice a few body weight accessory exercises like dips and pullups. These often take a lot more strength and endurance than people realize – especially big strength athletes who weigh closer to 300 lbs than 200 lbs (like me). That is a *lot* of weight to lift. On the other hand, even skinny small people have trouble with these exercises because let's face it – these exercises are difficult. Long story short, I've rarely met someone and started training with them and they were able to do four sets of ten reps. In fact, many people can't do *one* set of ten. If this is the case, set a rep goal of forty total reps. You may do ten reps the first time, then only seven – just keep grinding it out. Once you hit forty total reps, you are done. Your goal each week should be to increase the number of reps in each set, without necessarily exceeding forty total reps. Once you can do four sets of ten, then you can start adding reps to each set.

Finally, there are two lower body workouts per week. Because of this, there are two lower body workout templates – one that emphasizes squats, and one that emphasizes deadlifts. The accessory lifts are designed to complement the main lower body movement of the day. You may find yourself in a position where you cannot workout – or recover from – more than one lower body workout per week. This is completely normal. I have gone through months at a time where I could only do one lower body workout per week. If that is your case, just do one workout per week, and rotate between the two workouts. Your rep progression will change each week just as if you were doing the same workout. So week one, you will perform the "Lower Body (workout 1)" with week one reps and percentages, and the next week, you will perform the "Lower Body (workout 2)" with week two reps and percentages.

With those preliminaries out of the way, here is the program. After sharing the program, I will talk about progression in the program.

Monday - Upper Body

Bench Press

Week 1:	30% x 10 reps, 50% x 5 reps, 60% x 5 reps, 60% x 5 reps, 60% x 5 reps, 50% x rep max
Week 2:	30% x 10 reps, 50% x 5 reps, 65% x 5 reps, 65% x 5 reps, 65% x 5 reps, 50% x rep max
Week 3:	30% x 10 reps, 50% x 5 reps, 60% x 5 reps, 70% x 5 reps, 70% x 5 reps, 70% x 5 reps, 60% x rep max
Week 4:	30% x 10 reps, 50% x 5 reps, 60% x 5 reps,75% x 5 reps, 75% x 5 reps, 75% x 5 reps, 60% x rep max
Week 5:	30% x 10 reps, 50% x 5 reps, 60% x 5 reps,75% x 5 reps, 75% x 3 reps, 80% x 3 reps, 65% x rep max
Week 6:	30% x 10 reps, 50% x 5 reps, 60% x 5 reps,75% x 5 reps, 80% x 3 reps, 85% x 3 reps, 65% x rep max
Week 7:	30% x 10 reps, 50% x 5 reps, 60% x 5 reps,75% x 5 reps, 85% x 3 reps, 90% x 2 reps, 65% x rep max
Week 8:	30% x 10 reps, 50% x 5 reps, 60% x 5 reps,75% x 3 reps, 85% x 2 reps, 90% x 1 reps, 95% x rep max, 50% x 5 reps
Week 9:	Deload : 4 sets of ten reps

Close grip bench press

4 sets of 10

Dips

30-50 reps

Rear lateral raises

4 sets of 10

Lying triceps extensions

4 sets of 10

Tuesday - Lower Body (workout 1)

Squats

Week 1:	30% x 10 reps, 50% x 5 reps, 60% x 5 reps, 60% x 5 reps, 60% x 5 reps, 50% x rep max
Week 2:	30% x 10 reps, 50% x 5 reps, 65% x 5 reps, 65% x 5 reps, 65% x 5 reps, 50% x rep max
Week 3:	30% x 10 reps, 50% x 5 reps, 60% x 5 reps, 70% x 5 reps, 70% x 5 reps, 70% x 5 reps, 60% x rep max
Week 4:	30% x 10 reps, 50% x 5 reps, 60% x 5 reps,75% x 5 reps, 75% x 5 reps, 75% x 5 reps, 60% x rep max
Week 5:	30% x 10 reps, 50% x 5 reps, 60% x 5 reps,75% x 5 reps, 75% x 3 reps, 80% x 3 reps, 65% x rep max
Week 6:	30% x 10 reps, 50% x 5 reps, 60% x 5 reps,75% x 5 reps, 80% x 3 reps, 85% x 3 reps, 65% x rep max
Week 7:	30% x 10 reps, 50% x 5 reps, 60% x 5 reps,75% x 5 reps, 85% x 3 reps, 90% x 2 reps, 65% x rep max
Week 8:	30% x 10 reps, 50% x 5 reps, 60% x 5 reps,75% x 3 reps, 85% x 2 reps, 90% x 1 reps, 95% x rep max, 50% x 5 reps
Week 9:	Deload : 4 sets of ten reps

Glute-Ham Extensions

30-50 reps

Farmer's walk

30-50 steps

Calf raise

5 sets of 10-20

Hanging leg raises

30-50 reps

Thursday- Upper Body

Overhead Press

Week 1:	30% x 10 reps, 50% x 5 reps, 60% x 5 reps, 60% x 5 reps, 60% x 5 reps, 50% x rep max
Week 2:	30% x 10 reps, 50% x 5 reps, 65% x 5 reps, 65% x 5 reps, 65% x 5 reps, 50% x rep max
Week 3:	30% x 10 reps, 50% x 5 reps, 60% x 5 reps, 70% x 5 reps, 70% x 5 reps, 70% x 5 reps, 60% x rep max
Week 4:	30% x 10 reps, 50% x 5 reps, 60% x 5 reps,75% x 5 reps, 75% x 5 reps, 75% x 5 reps, 60% x rep max
Week 5:	30% x 10 reps, 50% x 5 reps, 60% x 5 reps,75% x 5 reps, 75% x 3 reps, 80% x 3 reps, 65% x rep max
Week 6:	30% x 10 reps, 50% x 5 reps, 60% x 5 reps,75% x 5 reps, 80% x 3 reps, 85% x 3 reps, 65% x rep max
Week 7:	30% x 10 reps, 50% x 5 reps, 60% x 5 reps,75% x 5 reps, 85% x 3 reps, 90% x 2 reps, 65% x rep max
Week 8:	30% x 10 reps, 50% x 5 reps, 60% x 5 reps,75% x 3 reps, 85% x 2 reps, 90% x 1 reps, 95% x rep max, 50% x 5 reps
Week 9:	Deload : 4 sets of ten reps

Bench Variant
4 sets of 10

DB shrugs
4 sets of 10

Dips
30-50 reps

Curls
4 sets of 10

Friday - Lower Body (workout 2)

Deadlift

Week 1:	30% x 10 reps, 50% x 5 reps, 60% x 5 reps, 60% x 5 reps, 60% x 5 reps, 50% x rep max
Week 2:	30% x 10 reps, 50% x 5 reps, 65% x 5 reps, 65% x 5 reps, 65% x 5 reps, 50% x rep max
Week 3:	30% x 10 reps, 50% x 5 reps, 60% x 5 reps, 70% x 5 reps, 70% x 5 reps, 70% x 5 reps, 60% x rep max
Week 4:	30% x 10 reps, 50% x 5 reps, 60% x 5 reps,75% x 5 reps, 75% x 5 reps, 75% x 5 reps, 60% x rep max
Week 5:	30% x 10 reps, 50% x 5 reps, 60% x 5 reps,75% x 5 reps, 75% x 3 reps, 80% x 3 reps, 65% x rep max
Week 6:	30% x 10 reps, 50% x 5 reps, 60% x 5 reps,75% x 5 reps, 80% x 3 reps, 85% x 3 reps, 65% x rep max
Week 7:	30% x 10 reps, 50% x 5 reps, 60% x 5 reps,75% x 5 reps, 85% x 3 reps, 90% x 2 reps, 65% x rep max
Week 8:	30% x 10 reps, 50% x 5 reps, 60% x 5 reps,75% x 3 reps, 85% x 2 reps, 90% x 1 reps, 95% x rep max, 50% x 5 reps
Week 9:	Deload : 4 sets of ten reps

Leg press
4 sets of 10-20

Kroc rows
4 sets of 8-20

Wide pulldowns or chinups
30-50 reps

Decline situps
30-50 reps

Progressing in the Program

First, I want to stress again that the percentages listed in the Nephilim Barbell Program are percentages of calculated max. You will notice that the plan calls for repping 95% of your calculated max every eighth week. This may sound like a lot, but it isn't. In fact, I have lifted at 95% of calculated max every week for months at a time. However, I never grew as fast lifting like that than cycling up to that weight as in the Nephilim Barbell Program. In reality, the only way to lift more weight is to lift more weight, but you have to give your body time to recover. You have to trigger resistance very near to your max in order to increase your max. I have been using this program for years, and never suffered fatigue or plateau. You can do it. However, if you do not include the volume and variety of accessory work included in this program, you may have to ramp it up.

Progression, however, is very, very simple in the Nephilim Barbell Program. Use the reps on week eight to recalculate your 1RM. That's pretty simple. So let's say you calculate your 1RM at 315 lbs. For your final set, you lift 95% of 315, which comes out to 299.25 lbs., which you round up to 300 lbs. You perform three reps. You now re-calculate your 1RM based off of that performance: $((3/30)+1)*300 = 330$. So your new 1RM is 330, and next cycle you will perform your heavy set at 313.5 lbs. Using this method I have added weight every cycle for more than a year in a row. However, consider the math: if you start at 225 max on a lift and perform three reps every eighth week, you will increase that lift to almost 400 lbs. in one year. If you perform two reps every eighth week, you will increase that lift to about 335 lbs. Now if you are normal, you won't hit multiple reps every eighth week. At some point you will only hit one rep on week eight. If that is the case, do not rest on your laurels. Just add ten pounds to your 1RM and go with it. What I have found is that people who are just starting out their journey are often able to perform multiple reps on their final set. People who are much stronger are often unable to perform more than one rep. This makes sense from a physiological standpoint – three reps at 225 is a lot less taxing than one rep at 545, let alone two reps. If you get to the point where you are lifting so much weight that you can never hit more than one rep, then it is time to switch to the drop set calculation. To do this, work up to 80% and preform as many reps as possible. To be clear, you will have to perform nine reps in order to calculate a new 1RM. If you do perform nine reps, at a max of 545 (which means lifting 9 reps at 435 lbs.) your new 1RM will be 566 – about 20 lbs. heavier. Eight reps, however, will just break even. This is just how the math works. A lot of strength athletes develop a non-linear strength limit as they get stronger, so lifting 80% for ten reps is easier than lifting 95% for two reps. However, if you were to lift 80% for ten reps, your new 1RM would calculate to 580 lbs – an increase of 35 lbs! That is a very highly unlikely increase. All of that to say that as you get stronger, you will have to use a combination of real world strength and brains to come up with a reasonable 1RM increase. As I have gotten stronger I have often simply increased my lifting weight by five pounds on every exercise for the next cycle. The important principle here is to keep progressing even when the mathematical model no longer fits your real world results.

A new 1RM max is not the only gain you can make, however. In fact, I want you to set the goal of setting a new PR in the gym *every single workout*. That's right, and it can be done. As you get stronger, it will get harder, but I am still setting at least one PR per week, every week. The first type of progression is what we just looked at – increasing your max. However, there are two other ways you can make gains. The first is to increase the number of reps in your final drop down set. So at the end of your working sets, the goal would be to do more reps in your final light set than you did the prior week. The third type of progression you can pursue is to reduce the amount of time it takes you to complete the work. All three of these methods increase your work capacity.

All three of these methods also require you to be disciplined and keep meticulous records. Keep a gym log. It doesn't have to be fancy – for years I just scratched my info onto an index card. A notebook is probably better so you can see a historical record, and once you start to take yourself seriously, you will probably choose to transcribe your notebook into a spreadsheet, so you can do some data modeling on your computer. Think I'm joking? Try running a regression analysis or gains graph on one years' worth of lifting data and you will be hooked. It is also a great motivator to see how far you have progressed in a year.

Now to clear up a few things about the percentages. You will notice that sometimes your percentages come out screwy – like 221.7 lbs. If your gym has pussy plates (2.5 lbs), then you can get to the nearest 5 lbs. Some gyms you will force you to round to the nearest 10 lbs. That is ok; just pick a number and stick to it. The point is to be consistent. So in the case above, 221.7 lbs. could be rounded to 225 lbs. or rounded to 215 lbs. I'd probably round it up because it is easier to load four 45s on the bar, but the choice is yours. The point is, write it down and use the same weight next week. That will keep you – and your gains – consistent. Now, it may be easy for you to remember what weight you chose for your final heavy set, but keep in mind that you are calculating percentages for all your sets. Don't be that idiot who thinks there is a difference between 5 reps at exactly 65% of your 1Rm, and rounding to the nearest 5 lbs. There's not. Just make sure you write it down so that if you round up this week you round up next week too.

Deload

Deload refers to a period of time when you do not lift heavy. The Nephilim Barbell Program is designed to have one deload week every eight weeks. On your deload week, you will only perform the Big Four, and you will do four sets of ten reps. I recommend no one go above 50% on these, but I hesitate to put a firm number out there because the point is to work on the groove and flood the muscles with blood (muscle food) – not to stress the muscle. You may have to do the motions with an empty bar. That's ok! Do lots of mobility work and static stretching. Do cardio. Do not perform accessory lifts. Your body needs time to heal. Your muscles may feel fine (I can't remember the last deload where I thought 'man, I need a break'), but your central nervous system needs time to heal. So does your mind. Back off the intensity for a week. You need a program that is sustainable for a decade if you want to be really strong, so take regularly scheduled time to chill and relax. The dude abides.

Lifting Methodology

It isn't enough to just move weights. I can't stress this enough, because the lifting methods presented in this chapter are just as important as any other part of the Nephilim Barbell Program. Part of strength training lifting methodology is built right into the program – the frequency of lifting and the percent of 1RM for example. However, there remains the methodology for *actually moving the weight*. In other words, how you move the weight influences the gains you make. Below are several methodologies that need to be worked into every workout. Each method includes instructions, but follow the general guideline: use CAT for all Big Four working sets, and choose ONE other methodology to practice for that particular workout. Mix it up, try not to do the same thing twice, and keep your body guessing.

Compensatory Acceleration Training (CAT)

Compensatory Acceleration Training, or CAT, is quite simply moving the weight with maximal force throughout the rep range. There are a few things that go into this – first, as a lift commences, leverages improve. Using simple physics, it is easy to see that if the speed stays the same throughout the lift, then less effort is being exerted at the top of the lift. CAT compensates for this improved leverage by increasing force. Second, many people "bounce" the weight at the bottom – for example, bouncing the weight off their chest, or bouncing their squat out of the hole. There is nothing wrong with using bounce provided it is allowed and you can perform it safely. However, it is specifically designed to *reduce* the amount of force necessary to move the weight. For CAT to work properly, you need to pause the weight, at least for a split second, before reversing it. Finally, remember that the contraction close to lockout is possibly the most important part of the motion. This work does not benefit from the stretch-shortening cycle like pushing out of the hole does. If this is the first you've heard of CAT you might be tempted to conflate it with speed work. Don't. CAT is about providing maximal force against the bar throughout the entire rep range. This won't always translate into a noticeable speed increase, especially at heavier weights. It will, however, result in a noticeable fatigue increase. Finally, be careful to perform the negative (downward portion, or eccentric movement) in a controlled fashion. Never let the weight just drop. This will actually make you much stronger, as more muscle fibers will be recruited, and your slow oxidative fibers will fatigue, allowing your IIb fibers to provide explosive concentric power. I imagine my negative as a fuse burning down; when I reach the bottom of the lift I visualize an explosion of TNT, forcing the weight up as violently as possible. Many strength athletes find similar visualization helpful.

Use CAT for all working sets of the Big Four exercises. Do NOT use CAT for your warmup sets (anything below 60% 1RM). You might be surprised to learn that I don't recommend using CAT for every exercise. It is very taxing on the central nervous system, and is best reserved for the Big Four.

Supersets

A superset is a training method where one set of exercise A is followed immediately by one set of exercise B. For this to work effectively, Exercise B needs to be a different kind of exercise than exercise A. Try opposing muscle groups for best results. For example, you wouldn't want to superset narrow grip bench presses with dips – both work out your triceps. You could, however, superset dips with rear lateral raises. Supersets are a great way to increase your cardiorespiratory system without overtaxing any one muscle group. It also cuts down your gym time, which is generally positive.

Dropsets

A dropset consists of completing a set, then reducing the weight and performing another set with no pause. One way to practice this is to perform one set of a given exercise – say, leg presses – then perform three more sets as a dropset. So you might perform one set at 275, then perform a dropset at 315, 275, 255.

Please note that in order for this to work, you really have to hit your rep target first, then drop weight. For example, doing ten reps at 100 lbs., followed by 5 reps at 60 lbs. This essentially adds more work on top of your planned work. This will create significantly different results from going up to, say, 150 lbs. for 5 reps, followed by 100 lbs. at 5 reps, followed by 50 lbs. at 5 reps. The first workout will stimulate hyperplasia, the second will promote hypertrophy. Keep in mind that the point of your accessory work is to stimulate hyperplasia; the Big Four take care of hypertrophy.

Pause Lifts

Pause lifts are an essential part of getting stronger. All of the Big Four should be performed with a pause at least once per cycle. A pause lift consists of setting up your equipment such that the weight is supported at the bottom. For squats you will often see this as a box, but setting up pins in the power rack also works. This is also the setup for a pause bench press. Pausing reduces your power significantly, so you will have to use lighter weight. I recommend that one of the first four weeks of the cycle be dedicated to pause pressing the Big Four. Pause pressing is less effective on accessory work because accessory motions are often bodyweight exercises or isolation exercises. This methodology is best saved for the Big Four.

Slow Lifts

Slow lifts are exactly what they sound like. Lift the weight slowly. I recommend that this method only be applied to accessory work. Use control, use lighter weight (it is much harder than it sounds), and be careful not to hitch or lose your momentum. Slow lifting mimics isometric contraction, which is a significant method for keeping your muscles growing.

Variable Leverage

Variable leverage refers to changing the levers involved in a lift. A classic example is wide-grip bench press. The wide grip bench press is a great way to increase your pressing strength. If you are targeting your press for improvement, try to incorporate wide grip pressing into your workouts. Another example is changing your grip width and pronation for pullup exercises. Try to vary your accessory lift leverage every once in a while. This doesn't have to be a change for an entire workout or cycle – for example, if you are performing pullups, you can change your grip every set every week if you want to. I do recommend wide grip bench presses to maximize strength, but again, use this methodology on one of your volume weeks. Varying the leverage in your squat and deadlift can be more tricky. Front squats, for example, can change the squat dynamic. You can try a wider grip deadlift, but I don't recommend it, as this puts more stress on your biceps flexors. Another option is sumo deadlift, which I also don't recommend since the mechanics are more technical. Instead, try Romanian deadlifts to mix up the leverages.

Burnouts

A burnout is generally an exercise performed with very high-rep sets. This may take the form of a drop set, or might just use really light weight. The purpose of a burnout is to really pump blood into the muscle. Blood is muscle food, and burnouts are a great way to help muscles grow. One exercise where I frequently use burnouts is biceps curls. I'll put a very low amount of weight on a cambered bar, and then curl away. I generally go for 30 to 50 reps a set, and perform two or three sets. About once every three months I will perform the mother of all burnout workouts. I got this from Janae Marie Kroc, and it remains one of may favorite workouts that I love to hate. It is an arm workout that incorporates 1,000 reps. Each set is a superset of 20 biceps reps and 20 triceps reps. It hurts. This is probably too extreme for most folks, but working in one burnout per week is probably good idea.

Accessory Work

The Big Four are supported and improved with the help of accessory work. I hate the term "accessory work" because it makes it sound like accessory work has all the useful qualities of a $2,000 purse or fluffy rat dog. In actuality, accessory work is an essential part of getting stronger. Below I will walk through the accessory exercises with some commentary on how to perform them effectively.

Close Grip Bench Press

The close grip bench press is a great way to polish off chest work while hammering the triceps. A few tips to maximize this exercise: first, grip the bar just where the knurling starts. Any narrower and you will risk slipping and also put more stress on your wrists. Any wider and it just turns into a regular bench press. Lower the bar until your elbow just breaks 90 degrees, then reverse the bar path. You shouldn't be touching your chest with this motion unless you have the build of Eric Spoto. You can use pause pressing technique on this if you desire, and drop sets work very well also. However, I don't recommend supersetting with any other exercise, as the narrow grip press takes a lot out of you.

Dips

Dips, specifically parallel bar dips, are the king of upper body accessory exercises. They work out the chest, shoulders, and triceps. A few

tips: for starters, go deep – you want to work out your entire upper yoke area. Second, lock out at the top – the long head of your triceps is only engaged when you are pulling your arm closer to the rear. If the angle between your sagittal plane and your upper arm never changes, then one-third of your triceps isn't working. You can weight these if you want, but I'd rather see good form without weight than bad form with weight.

Rear lateral raise

The fact is, your upper back and shoulder area takes a *ton* of work to develop. The reason is simple – there are a ton of muscles back there, and fatiguing them to the point of growth just flat out takes a lot of work. Rear laterals can help with this. Rear laterals need to be performed with very light weight while squeezing the muscles of the shoulder and upper back. The temptation is to swing the weights. We call that "ego lifting". Drop the weight, get a proper contraction, feel the burn. You're welcome.

Rear laterals should be performed bent over (or seated). Don't lock the elbow, don't swing the weights, and don't jerk your back. Imagine this motion as ripping open the gates of Troy.

Ripp extensions

These are just lying triceps extensions, but I call them Ripp extensions after Mark Rippetoe. In his version of the famous "skull crusher", the weight is lowered toward the forehead, but then continues behind the head until it is between the middle and the back of your head. This extra extension allows the long head of your triceps to become involved, since the starting motion will involve moving your elbows toward your groin. Perform these like you are trying to throw the weight at the ceiling.

Starting position for Ripp extensions utilizing the narrow grip on the EZ-Curl bar.

Bottom position with bar lowered behind head. This forces the long head of the triceps to engage. This lift should feel like you are throwing the barbell at the ceiling.

GH extensions

It is impossible to describe these in text – look up a video online or something. I always do a full back extension when I perform these, but I am careful not to let that turn into a swinging motion. I want my hammies to work.

Farmer's walk

Grab heavy shit. Walk with it.

World renowned strongman Bill Kazmaier doing the farmer's walk.

Calf Raise

Your calves are one of those interesting muscles that exist almost entirely to help your other muscles work. They are sort of like forearms in that regard. Never straighten your legs while doing these, and remember that you only really work your calves at the top of the contraction. Use lighter weight, and focus on the squeeze at the top. If you are wondering how calf raises help your strength goals, I'll tell you. Calf raises improve the flexibility and stability of your ankle tendons, as well as their strength. They are one of the most important exercises for maintaining lower body health over time, so don't neglect them.

Leg Raise

This is the mother of all abdominal exercises. This exercise is set up with a rep target, and don't be surprised if you can't hit it when you first start out. This might explain why you aren't seeing gains – your core is weak. Just keep at it; you will be surprised how quickly you get stronger. I generally perform three sets of 15.

Bench Variant

In order to press more, you have to press more. The bench variant accessory can be changed every week, or every cycle, or you can choose an exercise that

Wide grip incline barbell press used as a bench variant for accessory work.

complements your current weakness. Some common bench variants include the floor press, the rack press or pause press, the wide grip press, dumbbell presses, or any other bench press variant. It even includes bands or chains. There are only two rules when selecting a bench variant. First, this is NOT a heavy lifting set. This is accessory work, and the goal is to pump your pressing muscles full of blood. Blood is muscle food. Remember, Big Four for hypertrophy, accessory work for hyperplasia. Second, don't just do a regular bench press with less weight. This is not speed work, nor "greasing the groove". This should be a *complementary* exercise that works the muscle differently.

The floor press is a bench press where you lie on the floor. As such, your arms touch the ground at the bottom, and the motion ends up incorporating the pause press methodology by physics. Do not think of this as a sticking point exercise – science shows that working on your "sticking point" doesn't actually do anything. However, this exercise does remove the stretch-shortening cycle, meaning that it will work on raw, explosive power in the lockout portion of the press. The gains from this accessory lift carry over to the overhead press as well.

The rack press or pause press sets the barbell up on the safety bars of a power rack at the bottom position. You wriggle underneath the bar, then press it up. At the bottom, you rest it back on the safety bars. This is a fantastic exercise for building explosive strength out of the bottom of your pressing exercises.

Incline dumbbell pause presses are another great pressing exercise. Pause at the bottom, and use Compensatory Acceleration Training to complete the technique.

Shrugs

The shrug is one of the most abused lifts in the gym. Every week I see knuckleheads in the gym using way too much weight and a ROM of about 2 inches and calling them shrugs. Hogwash. There are two types of shrugs you can perform to help you improve your strength. The first is the power shrug. This is performed like a power clean, except you slap your traps together at the top instead of cleaning the weight. The other is the dumbbell shrug. Remember that you have to squeeze your traps together at the rear where they meet – not in the middle of your head. I see some people trying to shrug their shoulders into their ears. Stop it. Instead, hunch over slightly and let your traps contract *behind your head*. Use light enough weight that you can actually do the motion.

Another alternative is to use a smith machine. The physics of this machine allow you to incorporate lean into the motion. Just remember to work out the traps, and not turn this into an ego lift.

Curls

Curls in a strength training program? Yes, dammit. You have to have strong biceps to have a strong deadlift, lift a heavy atlas stone, or pull a jet on a rope. Vary your grip, squeeze at the top, and never ever use momentum to cheat. Lower the weight and do them right.

Leg Press

The leg press is a fantastic accessory because it mimics the squat while putting less strain on your lower back. Use light weight and a full range of motion to maximize effectiveness.

Kroc rows

These are named after Janea Marie Kroc. These look really similar to one arm dumbbell rows, but are completely different, so don't mistake one for the other. One of the main differences is that Kroc rows primarily work out your grip strength and your upper back yoke. One arm dumbbell rows primarily work out your lats. Here are the principles I use to maximize Kroc rows: first, the elbow moves out farther from the body than with a one arm dumbbell row. This allows the rear deltoid, rhomboid, infraspinatus, teres minor, and trapezius to engage more than the lats. Second, rest the weight on the floor at the bottom of every rep. Third, explode off the floor with these. I rarely use straps with these unless I am going super heavy as the goal is to improve grip strength. Generally, if I go above 150 lbs for reps I will use straps.

Wide pulldowns or chin-ups

I prefer pullup variations, but often after completing Kroc rows I am just too beat to heft my 265 lb. frame up and down like that. If I find myself fatigued – or even if I don't sometimes – I perform pulldowns instead. I vary the grip a lot on these. One of my favorites is the supinated (palms-up) narrow-grip pulldown. I got these from watching Dorian Yates train, and they remain a favorite of mine to this day. Another option is to use a weighted pullup assist machine. These have the benefit of reducing the negative, while allowing the same full-body engagement as a regular pullup.

Decline sit-up

This is another gut-blaster. Just do them, and be careful about cramps.

Cardio

Cardio is an important part of the Nephilim Barbell Program. I do cardio twice a week – both on my off days. I recommend high intensity interval training (HIIT) for your cardio. HIIT allows you to maximize your cardio while risking minimal injury. It also does not interfere with your muscle building the way other forms of cardio training tend to do. It is very easy to add HIIT to your gym workout. Get on an elliptical or treadmill. Warmup with a light jog, then sprint all out for 30 seconds. Return to walking or slow jogging speed for four minutes. The goal is to get your heart rate back down close to resting rate. Continue the four minute jog/30 second sprint for four cycles. Do this twice a week on your day off and follow your nutrition programming the same way you would for weight training. After a month or so, increase to five cycles. Eventually you will work up to eight cycle per workout. This is still barely 40 minutes with warmup and cool-down, so it isn't an especially vigorous commitment. It will, however, allow you to lift heavier weight and not gas out if you choose to compete.

Workout Alternatives

Making the Program Work for You

One of the most common concerns I hear is from people who are worried that they can't fit the entire Nephilim Barbell Program into their life, and are afraid they won't make the gains they want. If this is you; relax. Even I can't sustain this program indefinitely. Real life inevitably gets in the way, and I find my resources taxed. The most commonly taxed resource is time, but you may also go through periods where gym access, sleep, nutrition, or other resources are compromised. Below I have listed some alternatives that may help with these constraints.

Three Days a Week

If time or recuperation are scarce commodities, consider switching to only three workouts per week. To do this, perform a single lower body workout on Wednesday. Switch back and forth between the two lower body workouts, while progressing in the weight and reps as if you were following the same workout each week. So on week one you would perform workout one with three working sets of squats at 5 x 60%. On week two, you would perform workout two with three working sets of deadlifts at 5 x 65%. Don't worry; the Nephilim Barbell Program has been specifically engineered to allow this. However, there are two things you are giving up by switching to three days a week. The most obvious is calorie burn. If you are a hard gainer, this may be a blessing in disguise; burning less calories without adjusting your calories down could lead to unexpected growth. However, many folks find that three days a week of lifting affects their appetite, which affects their diet, which ends up negatively impacting their gains. The second thing you are giving up is the pace at which your cardiorespiratory and musculoskeletal systems develop. You don't grow twice as fast by working out your lower body twice a week, but you do grow faster.

This is also a great option if you are experiencing lower back pain or are recovering from any kind of injury. "Lower" body workouts are actually poorly named, because both the squat and the deadlift tax your entire body. If you are recovering from an injury, four workouts a week is probably too much. I have personally used this schedule many times when work interfered with the ability to do four workouts per week.

Limited Time

Often, you may find yourself in the gym with only thirty minutes or so to work out. Don't worry; it happens to the best of us. No matter how your time resource is constrained, always keep one principle in mind: the Big Four are the most important lifts to perform. Period. So maybe you can hit the gym four times a week, but only for twenty minutes or so? Warmup, perform the Big Four of the day (hey, I might be onto something there...in a few months you'll see skinny yuppies sporting BFOD branded water bottles and key fobs at the local fitness palace). If you still have time after this, dedicate it to a high-repetition motion that is the opposite of the Big Four motion you just performed. Just hammered out Bench Presses? Do Kroc rows. Shoulder Press? Pulldowns or chins. Deadlift? Dips. Squats? Ab work and biceps. Another alternative is to just list out your accessory work, and go through them one exercise at a time. Just pick up wherever you left off the next time you work out.

Cardio

I don't know what the big deal is with cardio. People hate it. Hell, *I* hate it. But I do it because it is an essential part of my game. The Nephilim Barbell Program incorporates cardio in two different ways. The first is by limiting the rest periods between accessory sets. Things like limiting rest to 180 seconds and super-setting opposing exercises already improve cardio. On top of that, the Nephilim Barbell Program recommends two HIIT cardio sessions per week. I perform these on my non weightlifting days. I can do these at home on my treadmill, so I don't count this as a workout. However, many people don't have time for this or would like to experience other forms of exercise. I can relate to this. I hate the indoors; all of my best training is done outside. Feel free to improvise on cardio – hiking, fartlek, kayaking, or just doing HIIT outside while running is a great opportunity to enjoy the great outdoors while meeting your fitness goals. Just keep in mind that HIIT has a significant advantage – it can burn calories and surface fat without depleting muscle size and strength. Most cardio doesn't do this. The reason the Nephilim Barbell Program relies on HIIT training is that it helps to keep belly fat off without restricting gains. This is a tactical choice – the Nephilim Barbell Program is NOT a "look good naked" program. It is about getting really strong. Belly fat, however, limits cardio, endurance, and mobility. Some belly (a "power belly") is good; it actually makes you stronger and works as a brace while squatting, moving atlas stones, etc. But too much fat is a hindrance.

Accessory Exercises

The accessory work selected for the Nephilim Barbell Program is designed to be complementary, so I don't recommend that beginners mess around with it too much. Having said that, there are no rules. Feel free to incorporate different exercises and movements into your work. I do this all the time – I may include different kinds of curls, or barbell rows, or upright rows, or dumbbell hang cleans, or one arm dumbbell clean and press…you get the picture. A lot of this has to do with how my body is developing. Many folks have to modify their accessory work due to time constraints. If you routinely don't have enough time to finish your workouts, consider pairing your Big Four workout with body weight accessory work. Dips, chin-ups, crunches, and back extensions are all healthy, multi-joint movements that will support your strength goals.

Strongman Training

If you can incorporate strongman training, do it! I love strongman training for its usefulness and comprehensive impact. I am probably one of a handful of people in the whole world that has a 250 lb. atlas stone and a couple of heavy chains in my back yard. The kids go out to play in the sand-box; daddy goes outside and lifts heavy shit. Sometimes I just walk around and play with the kids with 50 lbs. of chain around my neck.

Consider the following strongman exercises as being particularly effective.

Sled/prowler: Basically, this is just some kind of skis with weights on top. You push or pull it. Depending on setup, this can emphasize different muscle groups or mimic different strongman events. It is quite the burn, will toast your entire body, and is great for cardio.

Log lift: The log lift has two aspects which make it an ideal development tool for pressing strength. The first is the size – it is just plain difficult to lift. The second is that the grip is "neutral", which makes the motion slightly different. This is a great full-body workout.

Keg lift: This is not the same as a keg toss. If you have the space to do a keg toss, more power to you. If not, consider the keg lift. Fill the keg with sand, or if you are particularly lustful of punishment, water. Cleaning the keg takes a sort of rolling motion that will do murder to your wrists; pressing it overhead while all that water slops around takes incredible core strength.

Atlas stone: The atlas stone is a fantastic strength tool. It works out your entire body, but it puts unusual stress on your biceps. Be sure to warm up properly.

Autoregulation

You hear this term thrown around the gym a lot. I'm really not sure who coined the phrase, because there isn't really anything "automatic" about autoregulation. Basically, autoregulation is the idea that as you improve your skill and knowledge, you will change your workout in real-time to maximize your gains. This is a real phenomenon – as you improve, you will almost certainly begin to change your workout depending on various factors that influence your workout. The problem that I have seen is a regiment of skinny noobs blabbing about "autoregulation" as an excuse to not finish their workout, or skip the difficult parts, or whatever. In the old days, when a loser's ego got in the way of his workout, he would claim an old sports injury. These days they claim autoreg. Whatever. You *need* to get to the stage where you are autoregulating. Just don't use it as an excuse.

Nutrition

The Big Secret

I remember picking up a copy of Flex magazine as a teen and seeing some ungodly-huge athlete on the cover and thinking, "Holy shit! Is that real?" I spent the next six months devouring training magazines. It didn't take me long to notice something peculiar. Every athlete had a different training routine, but they all had the same eating routine. The exact. Same. Routine. That was a clue to me about the role that food plays in weight-lifting. My suspicions were confirmed when two different Mr. Olympias made the same basic claim: bodybuilding is 90% diet. Fast forward a few years, and I wasn't even remotely interested in bodybuilding, but that little piece of advice stuck with me. To this day, I believe that diet is a huge factor in strength training. It certainly isn't 90% - in fact, if you are scaling by difficulty, then it isn't even 50/50. It is much easier (at least for me) to eat right than to bang away in the gym day after day. Nevertheless, without proper food, you will not meet your strength training goals. Let me say that again. Without proper food, you will not meet your strength training goals. Period. So follow along below as I outline the basics.

Food Types

The ugly truth is that as long as you consume enough calories from reasonable sources you will get strong with the Nephilim Barbell Program. And I do mean "ugly" truth, because you will probably start to look like something from Sea World. This will affect your performance. Make no mistake – being fat will inhibit your goals and gains. In fact, belly fat reduces testosterone. Fact. Fat is a relative term, of course. It is very difficult for anyone to maintain a six-pack and make any kind of real gains. It can be done, but rarely without some chemical help. Knowing what you are consuming is the first step to reaching your goals. I'm not going to get too technical in this chapter – my goal is for you to transform your life by transforming your eating habits, not for you to fall asleep reading a dissertation on performance nutrition.

Let's start with the basics: there is food, and then there are consumables. "Consumables" are things you can buy in the grocery store and put in your mouth. This includes everything from steak to gummy worms. "Food" on the other

hand comprises all those things that we actually evolved to eat for fuel. The Nephilim Barbell Program is designed around eating actual food. You can add consumables on top of the program, but be disciplined. Beer is awesome, but it suppresses testosterone production and is a bottle of nearly empty calories. Food is found in nature, and should be consumed as close to its natural state as possible. Use your brain here, though. Many vegetables are better consumed cooked: broccoli and carrots, for example, are much more nutritious when cooked by simple virtue of the fact that most people's gut can't break down the cellular wall structure when these veggies are eaten raw. Of course you should cook your grains as well, and if I have to tell you to cook your meat, then maybe this book is too advanced for you. Bottom line? It is ok to cook your food. However, avoid frying or anything obscene. So chicken, corn, and potatoes are all food. Fried chicken, corn fritters, and French fries are NOT food. Skip them.

Ok, now that we got the basics out of the way, I want you to think of food in four basic groups. These are Protein, Fat, Active Carbs, and Free Carbs. We will cover these in order. A quick note on carbs: any scheme to divide up carbs is essentially arbitrary. I like the terms "active" and "inactive" carbs because they define how the carbs work, rather than what "kind" they are. If there is a fifth group, it is water. Obviously this isn't a food, but you need to drink huge amounts of water. Seriously. Water is the vehicle that carries nutrients into your cells. Buy a gallon jug of water, and drink it in one day. Then refill it tomorrow and drink it again. It isn't magic, but it is essential to ensuring that your body repairs itself and cleans out all the junk that working out strips from your cells.

Protein is the most important food group. It is the building block of muscle. You probably know that already. There are 20 amino acids (proteins) that make up our bodies. Of these, nine are "essential". An essential amino acid is one that your body can not produce naturally – at some point in our distant past, the genes that enable production of these proteins broke, and that trait was passed down to us. Now we must consume these from the outside in order to live. The nine essential amino acids are (in alphabetic order) histidine, isoleucine, leucine, lysine, methionine, phenylalanine, threonine, tryptophan and valine. Remember, your body *cannot manufacture these*. You must consume them from outside sources. This is one reason why I highly recommend any vegan have a close conversation with their doctor before embarking on any weight training program. It is very, very difficult (and expensive) to get all these from plants alone (not to mention biologic availability; a subject for a different discussion). Proteins also jack up your metabolism – as much as 30% of protein calories are burned as heat.

Fat is the second most important food group. If you've ever heard any bullshit about low-fat food, forget it. Fat is essential. Humans couldn't even reproduce without it. Fat is essential for the operation of our central nervous system, holds vitamins (D, E, A, K), and is essential to blood production and brain function. You must eat fat! Where fat differs from protein and carbohydrates is that fat is almost twice as calorically dense. One gram of protein or carbs has 5 calories. One gram of fat has 9 calories. So if you wanted to eat an equal number of calories from fat, protein, and carbs, only 21% of your food volume could constitute fat. As well, there are "obvious" fats, like butter or cooking oil, and there are hidden fats, like the fats in peanuts, olives, or avocadoes. All of that is a fancy way of saying that you don't have to go out of your way to eat fat. In fact, I try to eat "lean" – I trim obvious fat from my steak, for example, and I don't cook things in oil very often. But I do eat the fat in eggs, butter, and all kinds of seeds and plants. I also supplement with a mercury free krill oil supplement. Bottom line? Try to avoid "bad" fats like any kind of man-made fat (hey, that isn't a food and shouldn't be on your diet anyway), but don't worry about fat that shows up in your food naturally. It's supposed to be there.

Carbohydrates are the most misunderstood of all food types. You MUST eat carbs. Period. PERIOD. Listen, fancy-pants, there wouldn't be a multi-million dollar fitness industry around cutting carbs if it worked. If it worked, we'd all be skinny and the industry would go out of business! Carbs provide the essential fuel for your workouts. Seriously – as you start to get stronger you will be able to tell a difference in your workout if you aren't getting the fuel you need. Especially if you are skinny – just fucking eat. I ate 10,000 calories a day for a full year. I started at 185 lbs., and ended at 255 lbs. I went from 12% body fat to 14% body fat. That's it. You can't see gains like that without eating. Now having said that, there are two types of carbs. The first is "active". These carbs are often called "high-glycemic" or maybe "simple" carbs. I like the term "active" because it describes what the carbs do – they fuel activity. Specifically, they increase blood sugar and insulin production. This is important because insulin is your alpha hormone. No, it doesn't make you aggressive (in fact, it will put you to sleep), instead, it grows muscle like nobody's business. Pretty much any carb that is not a vegetable is an active carb. Even beans, which are high in fiber, are generally active. Active carbs are the ones you need to watch out for. If you are gaining fat faster than you would like, the first thing I would do, once you ensure your diet is clean, is to reduce active carbs. Also, keep in mind that some active carbs are more useful than others. White rice is a very low-nutrient active carb. It is great for energy, and not much else. Beans, on the other hand, have numerous proteins and micro-nutrients besides sugars. So mix your active carbs up.

Inactive carbs (complex, fibrous, or free carbs) don't affect the production of blood sugar and insulin like active carbs. Here is the awesome, awesome secret of strength training: you can eat as many inactive carbs as you want. Yep. Squash, broccoli, kale, mushrooms, peppers – eat up, my hearties! You can even use this knowledge to mix a healthy amount of active carbs and fats up with monstrous amounts of inactive carbs and be full for hours (this gets more difficult as you get larger). For example, you can stuff bell peppers with minced mushrooms, carrots, cauliflower, green beans, and rice, and then drizzle with olive oil and bake. This tastes amazing, and about 75% of the calories are "free". Just don't over do it with the rice.

That's it, those are the four food types. Below we will talk about how much you should consume. Just remember, if your number one goal is getting stronger, then you need to eat as much as you can. Worry about getting pretty later; if you don't eat, you won't grow. Period.

Food Quantities

The most important rule here is that it is better to eat too much than too little. Too many people want to get insanely strong and still look like a fitness competitor at a meet. Have you ever seen those competitors back stage? As soon as the meet is over, they are stuffing their faces like it's the last supper. You have to eat. That being said, there is such a thing as eating too much, but it is much more common for strength athletes to be consuming too little of one thing or another. For protein, you want to consume at least one gram per pound of body weight per day. Actually, this is complete bullshit. Protein timing is more important than quantity (we'll cover timing below), and the more you weigh, the less this rule applies. Still, you want to consume at least 150 grams per day, although anything more than 300 grams is probably a waste. For ease of calculation, it is ok to just go with 1 gram per pound of body weight. For fat, you want one half gram per pound of bodyweight. For a 250 pound lifter, that would calculate out to 250 grams of protein and 125 grams of fat. That's a total calorie count of 2375. A 250 pound lifter needs at least 3,500 calories, so the rest – 160 grams – will come from carbs ((3500 – 2375)/5 = 160). In reality, I weigh around 275 lbs., and my diet is between 5,000 and 7,000 calories. I can get away with low calorie counts because of the way I time my food, but you will know if you are not eating enough. You will gas out in the gym. If your muscles tire before you are winded, then you aren't eating enough. Remember that chapter about muscle types? Your oxidative muscles are used first before your non-oxidative fibers are recruited; once your sugars drop, your muscles will fail. You always want your wind to give out before your muscles. There are all kinds of diet plans out there, so I won't bore you with details. Just eat enough and eat the right amounts of the right food.

Timing

First of all, eat like you get paid to. Think about it for a minute – you wake up, shit, shower, and shave, go to the office, and plan a healthy meal plan. You buy the ingredients, cook them, and then consume them. Not only do you get to eat your cooking, but you get paid to. If this were your job, how awesome would that be? Treat your diet like you get paid to do it right – because in a way, you do. You get paid in gains. Timing is just about as important to your gains as food quantity. For starters, you want to eat every three hours. That has been impossible for most of my adult life. Sorry, but I have a life to live. You are quite possibly in the same boat. So, here's the secret for those of us who can't eat every three hours: time your nutrition around your workout. There are reams and reams of recent science on how what we eat before, during, and after our workout affects recovery. Feel free to read it if you are a glutton for punishment. Or you can just take my advice. First, your nutrition around your workout needs to be liquid. Solid food often won't really help you out for hours or even days (seriously). Liquid food, however, is consumed very rapidly. Before you work out, consume a small amount of whey protein, sugar, and electrolytes. I use one scoop of whey, about a tablespoon of sugar, and a scoop of powdered electrolytes. You can buy pre-made pre-workout supplements, but I don't like them because they usually have caffeine. You can just use regular table sugar, but I use bulk dextrose in my shakes, as it is cheaper and absorbs better than table sugar (table sugar is actually sucrose, which will hydrolyze in the blood stream into fructose and glucose – in other words, it is less beneficial than dextrose).

My post-workout shake is substantial. It generally consists of 60 grams of whey protein, 40 grams of sugar, and added BCAAs. I also often take a vitamin complex. This shake must be consumed immediately after your workout. I sometimes start mine during my last exercise. Using the right nutrition timing around your workout allows your eating program to be much more effective, even if you can't get all your other meals timed just right – or at all.

You may also want to consider consuming nutrition during your workout. This can be done by mixing some protein and sugar and vitamins together for consumption while working out. You do not want to consume too much here; the purpose is to keep the muscles from getting over depleted, not to fill you up. I have tried intra-workout nutrition and I have tried pre- and post- nutrition only, and I can't tell a difference. My workouts rarely last longer than an hour, and I just don't get depleted enough for intra-workout nutrition to make much of a difference. Your mileage may vary.

Supplements

I'm not a huge fan of supplements – having said that, they are an essential part of getting big and strong. The most important supplements are the ones that go into my workout shakes – whey protein, dextrose, glutamine, leucine, electrolyte complex, and BCAA mix. I buy these in bulk to save money – they end up being cheaper than food. There are only two other supplements that I use on a regular basis. The first is creatine monohydrate. Creatine is an important tool in maximizing nutrient delivery – I highly recommend it. Creatine is a single-chain amino that is produced in the liver, and helps with bonding during ATP fuel cycle. Ensure that you are drinking enough water while taking it, and I always take about three months off a year from its use. This helps keep my body balanced and guessing. The other supplement I use regularly is a multi-vitamin complex. I want to stress that you absolutely do NOT need to use supplements to get big on the Nephilim Barbell Program. However, I will say that I have found it much easier to build mass if using liquid nutrition around my workouts.

Rest and Recovery

Everything we have talked about up to this point is all for nothing without the proper rest and recovery. Remember the General Adaptation Syndrome? You have to stress your muscles, then let them adapt. This takes time. There are four major parts of your recovery program, as outlined below. You cannot make gains without a well engineered and properly executed nutrition program, and you can't make gains without proper rest and recovery.

Sleep

You have to sleep. Sleep is how your muscles repair. The problem, of course, is that no one has time to sleep. So let's start with the ideal and go from there. Ideally, you will get 8-9 hours of sleep in every 24-hour period. This makes sense, biologically, since that is about how long the sun is down. However, keep in mind that "gathered sleep" – the practice of saving all your sleep for sundown – is a phenomenon that essentially post-dates the clock. One of the most common pre-modern sleeping habits was to go to bed at sundown, wake for an hour or two in the middle of the night, then go back to sleep. This was often paired with an afternoon nap, or siesta. So let's talk about your sleep schedule. Make getting sleep a priority. Manage your priorities, of course, but remember that sleep is essential to your physical, emotional, and mental health. On top of that, it is essential for muscle repair and recovery. If you can't get a full night's sleep, try taking a siesta. This may or may not be possible depending upon your life schedule. It usually takes about two weeks to properly adjust to a new sleep schedule, so you may have to struggle a while before your new sleep habits work for you. I caution against using any kind of sleep aid, but if you really struggle try natural supplements like valerian root. Most chemical sleep aids can cause serious disruptions of the sleep cycle. My current sleep schedule is 9pm (I go to bed at 8:30 to ensure I am asleep by 9) to 5am. That is 8 solid hours.

Last but not least, do not sleep in. Instead, set up a schedule that allows you to get proper sleep and stick with it every day. That means no sleeping in on Saturday, no staying up late on Friday, and – you guessed it – no partying. Put your health and your body first.

Mobility

I am so sick of this word. It seems like every internet yahoo and his brother is humping a foam roller and doing band pull-aparts and calling it mobility work. But the physiological reality is that working out damages your musculoskeletal system. As it repairs, it loses flexibility. A stiff musculoskeletal system means a lack of mobility. A lack of mobility means you can't do stuff like lift a log over your head, at least not without pulling something. So your job is to put that flexibility back. Mobility work has two main components – proactive and reactive.

Proactive mobility work is about getting your body into shape prior to lifting. You hear all kinds of nonsense these days about "warming up". Right now, static stretching is an evil beast that will kill your gains and turn you into a zucchini. Soon this fad will fade, and people will be rubbing sea salt on their hamstrings. Forget this nonsense. To reach your strength goals, you must be able to lift – for years. You have to stay healthy and lift with dedication for five or ten *years* to get really strong. That means you have to stay flexible, strong, and resilient. That means you have to have a robust system for maintaining your flexibility. Don't worry about reinventing the wheel here – strongman (and strongwoman) competitors have been lifting heavy shit for over fifty years. They know mobility, and the proof is in the pudding. One of the habits that strongmen and powerlifters around the globe share is that of proactive mobility. Proactive mobility is a daily mobility habit designed to keep you limber and athletic, and it consists primarily of static stretching. Yep. It's true. Forget the fad-hype bologna. Do what works. My proactive mobility work is built around a series of stretches that I learned in martial arts class. It works out the whole body, and keeps you limber enough to unleash a round-house kick on Chuck Norris' beard. I'd like to write this routine down, but it is just too complicated to write down. Hell, I don't even know what the movements are called. My recommendation is that you look up a full-body stretching routine and make it part of your day. I always wake up, drink a pint of water, get ready for my day, then do a full-body stretch. I drink the water first so my muscles are hydrated. You can also do some foam rolling or work with a lacrosse ball. I work out four days a week, and save my roller and ball for workout days. The other three days I just do static stretching.

Reactive mobility is designed specifically for your workout and has two parts; the part before the workout, and the part after. Before the workout, I follow Brandon Lilly's advice – stretch it, mash it, warm it. I start out with stretching the muscles I intend to use. Science indicates that stretching limits your strength. This is a good thing; it keeps you from damaging yourself. Do it. Then, I use a foam roller or lacrosse ball to mash up all the muscles I'm going to use. Finally, I use light weights to warm up the specific muscles I intend to use. At the end of the workout, I do the same thing in reverse order. There's no deep, dark secret here – you just have to do it. The foam and ball help to separate muscle fibers that bind together during the healing process. Repetitive, daily mobility work is far more effective than trying to limber up after letting yourself atrophy.

Having said that, some athletes choose to get an occasional deep tissue massage or other therapy to help them stay healthy. That's up to you. I have been doing regular stretching all my adult life and have had no issues. You can also try implementing some of the following methods for recovery. Ice bath: these help your muscles heal while also boosting testosterone production. I don't bathe in actual ice – I just run cold water into the tub and soak in it. Living in Minnesota, this is pretty close to bathing in a glacier. You can also try cold showers. Another recovery option is the classic Epsom salt bath. The choice is yours, but chances are, you don't have time for all that. I know I don't. What I do have time for is fifteen minutes a day to stretch. Make the time.

Cycling

Cycling (not bicycling) is the science of timing your workouts. Remember the primary principles of the Nephilim Barbell Program? One of them is proper periodization. Your body is designed to make gains this way. Think of your progression like waves lapping the shore – you can't just tidal wave to infinite gains. You have to cycle through peaks and valleys in order for your body to adapt and grow. This physiological reality is programmed into the Nephilim Barbell Program – every eight weeks you will peak your strength and then take a week off. From there, you will start the next wave. You should also consider cycling your nutrition. I often take a day off to fast (not only does this not kill your gains, it boosts testosterone production); sometimes I cycle through a high carb diet, other times I cycle a low carb diet (but never during a peak strength phase). Use the principle of cycling to keep your body guessing.

Nutrition

Nutrition is already covered in its own chapter, and I won't rehash that here. But it is only appropriate in a chapter on recovery to mention nutrition. You must have proper nutrition to recover. You must have proper nutrition to recover. You MUST have proper nutrition to recover.

Recap

The Nephilim Barbell Program is a combination of proper lifting, proper nutrition, and proper recovery. The principles and methods outlined in this book are designed around a normal lifestyle; you can have a normal balanced life and still accomplish amazing physical feats of strength. Just remember those three concepts, and it will keep you centered in life and in your workout routine. You have to balance life with lifting, and you have to balance your lifting among working out, eating, and resting. It really is that simple. Introduce some discipline into your life, set some lofty goals for yourself, and for gods' sake, train like a man of renown. Train like a Nephilim.

Training:
Periodized progression in the "Big Four" complemented with accessory lifts stimulate both hypertrophy and hyperplasia. Do cardio!

Nutrition:
Eat a lot of calories of actual food – no processed garbage. Consume a properly balanced liquid meal prior to working out, and a properly balanced liquid meal immediately upon completing your workout.

Recovery:
Be disciplined in your recovery. Strive for eight hours of gathered sleep per night. Work in a siesta if you can. Do mobility work and daily stretching. Remember that you have to stay healthy for years in order to reach your strength goals.

Bibliography

1.   Holloszy JO, Booth FW: Biochemical adaptations to endurance exercise in muscle. Annu Rev Physiol 1976, 38:273-291.

2.   Costill DL, Coyle EF, Fink WF, Lesmes GR, Witzmann FA: Adaptations in skeletal muscle following strength training. J Appl Physiol Respir Environ Exerc Physiol 1979, 46:96-99.

3.   Tesch PA, Larsson L: Muscle hypertrophy in bodybuilders. Eur J Appl Physiol Occup Physiol 1982, 49:301-306.

4.   Sola OM, Christensen DL, Martin AW: Hypertrophy and hyperplasia of adult chicken anterior latissimus dorsi muscles following stretch with and without denervation. Exp Neurol 1973, 41:76-100.

5.   Alway SE, Winchester PK, Davis ME, Gonyea WJ: Regionalized adaptations and muscle fiber proliferation in stretch-induced enlargement. J Appl Physiol (1985) 1989, 66:771-781.

6.   Alway SE, Gonyea WJ, Davis ME: Muscle fiber formation and fiber hypertrophy during the onset of stretch-overload. Am J Physiol 1990, 259:C92-102.

7.   Antonio J, Gonyea WJ: Ring fibres express ventricular myosin in stretch overloaded quail muscle. Acta Physiol Scand 1994, 152:429-430.

8.   Antonio J, Gonyea WJ: Muscle fiber splitting in stretch-enlarged avian muscle. Med Sci Sports Exerc 1994, 26:973-977.

9.   Antonio J, Gonyea WJ: Skeletal muscle fiber hyperplasia. Med Sci Sports Exerc 1993, 25:1333-1345.

10.   Antonio J, Gonyea WJ: Progressive stretch overload of skeletal muscle results in hypertrophy before hyperplasia. J Appl Physiol (1985) 1993, 75:1263-1271.

11.   Antonio J, Gonyea WJ: Role of muscle fiber hypertrophy and hyperplasia in intermittently stretched avian muscle. J Appl Physiol (1985) 1993, 74:1893-1898.

12.   Ashmore CR, Summers PJ: Stretch-induced growth in chicken wing muscles: myofibrillar proliferation. Am J Physiol 1981, 241:C93-97.

13.   Gollnick PD, Parsons D, Riedy M, Moore RL: Fiber number and size in overloaded chicken anterior latissimus dorsi muscle. J Appl Physiol Respir Environ Exerc Physiol 1983, 54:1292-1297.

14.   Barnett JG, Holly RG, Ashmore CR: Stretch-induced growth in chicken wing muscles: biochemical and morphological characterization. Am J Physiol 1980, 239:C39-46.

15.   Holly RG, Barnett JG, Ashmore CR, Taylor RG, Mole PA: Stretch-induced growth in chicken wing muscles: a new model of stretch hypertrophy. Am J Physiol 1980, 238:C62-71.

16.   Kennedy JM, Eisenberg BR, Reid SK, Sweeney LJ, Zak R: Nascent muscle fiber appearance in overloaded chicken slow-tonic muscle. Am J Anat 1988, 181:203-215.

17.   McCormick KM, Schultz E: Mechanisms of nascent fiber formation during avian skeletal muscle hypertrophy. Dev Biol 1992, 150:319-334.

18.   Winchester PK, Gonyea WJ: Regional injury and the terminal differentiation of satellite cells in stretched avian slow tonic muscle. Dev Biol 1992, 151:459-472.

19.   Winchester PK, Gonyea WJ: A quantitative study of satellite cells and myonuclei in stretched avian slow tonic muscle. Anat Rec 1992, 232:369-377.

20.   Winchester PK, Davis ME, Alway SE, Gonyea WJ: Satellite cell activation in the stretch-enlarged anterior latissimus dorsi muscle of the adult quail. Am J Physiol 1991, 260:C206-212.

21.   Armstrong RB, Marum P, Tullson P, Saubert CWt: Acute hypertrophic response of skeletal muscle to removal of synergists. J Appl Physiol Respir Environ Exerc Physiol 1979, 46:835-842.

22.   Chalmers GR, Roy RR, Edgerton VR: Variation and limitations in fiber enzymatic and size responses in hypertrophied muscle. J Appl Physiol (1985) 1992, 73:631-641.

23.   Giddings CJ, Gonyea WJ: Morphological observations supporting muscle fiber hyperplasia following weight-lifting exercise in cats. Anat Rec 1992, 233:178-195.

24.   Gollnick PD, Timson BF, Moore RL, Riedy M: Muscular enlargement and number of fibers in skeletal muscles of rats. J Appl Physiol Respir Environ Exerc Physiol 1981, 50:936-943.

25.   Mikesky AE, Giddings CJ, Matthews W, Gonyea WJ: Changes in muscle fiber size and composition in response to heavy-resistance exercise. Med Sci Sports Exerc 1991, 23:1042-1049.

26.   Alway SE, Grumbt WH, Gonyea WJ, Stray-Gundersen J: Contrasts in muscle and myofibers of elite male and female bodybuilders. J Appl Physiol (1985) 1989, 67:24-31.

27.   Giddings CJ, Neaves WB, Gonyea WJ: Muscle fiber necrosis and regeneration induced by prolonged weight-lifting exercise in the cat. Anat Rec 1985, 211:133-141.

28.   Gonyea WJ: Role of exercise in inducing increases in skeletal muscle fiber number. J Appl Physiol Respir Environ Exerc Physiol 1980, 48:421-426.

29.   Gonyea WJ: Muscle fiber splitting in trained and untrained animals. Exerc Sport Sci Rev 1980, 8:19-39.

30.   Gonyea WJ, Ericson GC: Morphological and histochemical organization of the flexor carpi radialis muscle in the cat. Am J Anat 1977, 148:329-344.

31.   Gonyea WJ, Ericson GC: An experimental model for the study of exercise-induced skeletal muscle hypertrophy. J Appl Physiol 1976, 40:630-633.

32.   Ho KW, Roy RR, Tweedle CD, Heusner WW, Van Huss WD, Carrow RE: Skeletal muscle fiber splitting with weight-lifting exercise in rats. Am J Anat 1980, 157:433-440.

33.   Gonyea WJ, Sale DG, Gonyea FB, Mikesky A: Exercise induced increases in muscle fiber number. Eur J Appl Physiol Occup Physiol 1986, 55:137-141.

34.   Tamaki T, Uchiyama S, Nakano S: A weight-lifting exercise model for inducing hypertrophy in the hindlimb muscles of rats. Med Sci Sports Exerc 1992, 24:881-886.

35.   Eddinger TJ, Moss RL, Cassens RG: Fiber number and type composition in extensor digitorum longus, soleus, and diaphragm muscles with aging in Fisher 344 rats. J Histochem Cytochem 1985, 33:1033-1041.

36.   Timson BF, Dudenhoeffer GA: The effect of severe dietary protein restriction on skeletal muscle fiber number, area and composition in weanling rats. J Anim Sci 1985, 61:416-422.

37.   Timson BF, Bowlin BK, Dudenhoeffer GA, George JB: Fiber number, area, and composition of mouse soleus muscle following enlargement. J Appl Physiol (1985) 1985, 58:619-624.

38.   Dudenhoeffer GA, Bowlin BK, Timson BF: A brief study of within litter and within strain variation in skeletal muscle fiber number in three lines of laboratory rodents. Growth 1985, 49:450-454.

39.   Vaughan HS, Goldspink G: Fibre number and fibre size in a surgically overloaded muscle. J Anat 1979, 129:293-303.

40.   Gonyea WJ: Fiber size distribution in the flexor carpi radialis muscle of the cat. Anat Rec 1979, 195:447-454.

41.   Mikesky, A. E., W. Matthews, C. J. Giddings, and W. J. Gonyea. Muscle enlargement and exercise performance in the cat. J. Appl. Sport Sci. Res. 3: 85-92, 1989.

42.   Yamada S, Buffinger N, DiMario J, Strohman RC: Fibroblast growth factor is stored in fiber extracellular matrix and plays a role in regulating muscle hypertrophy. Med Sci Sports Exerc 1989, 21:S173-180.

43.   Kennedy JM, Sweeney LJ, Gao LZ: Ventricular myosin expression in developing and regenerating muscle, cultured myotubes, and nascent myofibers of overloaded muscle in the chicken. Med Sci Sports Exerc 1989, 21:S187-197.

44.   Frenzel H, Schwartzkopff B, Reinecke P, Kamino K, Losse B: Evidence for muscle fiber hyperplasia in the septum of patients with hypertrophic obstructive cardiomyopathy (HOCM). Quantitative examination of endomyocardial biopsies (EMCB) and myectomy specimens. Z Kardiol 1987, 76 Suppl 3:14-19.

45.   Klein CS, Marsh GD, Petrella RJ, Rice CL: Muscle fiber number in the biceps brachii muscle of young and old men. Muscle Nerve 2003, 28:62-68.

46.   MacDougall JD, Sale DG, Alway SE, Sutton JR: Muscle fiber number in biceps brachii in bodybuilders and control subjects. J Appl Physiol Respir Environ Exerc Physiol 1984, 57:1399-1403.

47.   MacDougall JD, Sale DG, Elder GC, Sutton JR: Muscle ultrastructural characteristics of elite powerlifters and bodybuilders. Eur J Appl Physiol Occup Physiol 1982, 48:117-126.

48.   Nygaard, E. and E. Nielsen. Skeletal muscle fiber capillarisation with extreme endurance training in man. In Eriksson B, Furberg B (Eds).

Swimming Medicine IV(vol. 6, pp. 282-293). University Park Press, Baltimore, 1978.

49.   Larsson L, Tesch PA: Motor unit fibre density in extremely hypertrophied skeletal muscles in man. Electrophysiological signs of muscle fibre hyperplasia. Eur J Appl Physiol Occup Physiol 1986, 55:130-136.

50.   Haggmark T, Jansson E, Svane B: Cross-sectional area of the thigh muscle in man measured by computed tomography. Scand J Clin Lab Invest 1978, 38:355-360.

51.   Schantz P, Fox ER, Norgren P, Tyden A: The relationship between the mean muscle fibre area and the muscle cross-sectional area of the thigh in subjects with large differences in thigh girth. Acta Physiol Scand 1981, 113:537-539.

52.   Bischoff R: Interaction between satellite cells and skeletal muscle fibers. Development 1990, 109:943-952.

53.   Darr KC, Schultz E: Exercise-induced satellite cell activation in growing and mature skeletal muscle. J Appl Physiol (1985) 1987, 63:1816-1821.

54.   Cote C, Simoneau JA, Lagasse P, Boulay M, Thibault MC, Marcotte M, Bouchard C: Isokinetic strength training protocols: do they induce skeletal muscle fiber hypertrophy? Arch Phys Med Rehabil 1988, 69:281-285.

55.   Hather BM, Tesch PA, Buchanan P, Dudley GA: Influence of eccentric actions on skeletal muscle adaptations to resistance training. Acta Physiol Scand 1991, 143:177-185.

56.   Wong TS, Booth FW: Protein metabolism in rat tibialis anterior muscle after stimulated chronic eccentric exercise. J Appl Physiol (1985) 1990, 69:1718-1724.

57.   Wong TS, Booth FW: Protein metabolism in rat gastrocnemius muscle after stimulated chronic concentric exercise. J Appl Physiol (1985) 1990, 69:1709-1717.

58.   Carlson BM: The regeneration of skeletal muscle. A review. Am J Anat 1973, 137:119-149.

59.   MacDougall, J.D. Morphological changes in human skeletal muscle following strength training and immobilization. In: Human Muscle Power (pp. 269-288). N.L. Jones, N. McCartney, A. J. McComas (Eds.). Human Kinetics Publisher, Inc. Champaign, Illinois, 1986.

60.   Roman WJ, Alway SE: Stretch-induced transformations in myosin expression of quail anterior latissimus dorsi muscle. Med Sci Sports Exerc 1995, 27:1494-1499.

61.   Carson JA, Alway SE, Yamaguchi M: Time course of hypertrophic adaptations of the anterior latissimus dorsi muscle to stretch overload in aged Japanese quail. J Gerontol A Biol Sci Med Sci 1995, 50:B391-398.

62.   Carson JA, Yamaguchi M, Alway SE: Hypertrophy and proliferation of skeletal muscle fibers from aged quail. J Appl Physiol (1985) 1995, 78:293-299.

63.   Alway SE: Stretch induces non-uniform isomyosin expression in the quail anterior latissimus dorsi muscle. Anat Rec 1993, 237:1-7.

64.   Alway SE: Perpetuation of muscle fibers after removal of stretch in the Japanese quail. Am J Physiol 1991, 260:C400-408.

65.   Sjostrom M, Lexell J, Eriksson A, Taylor CC: Evidence of fibre hyperplasia in human skeletal muscles from healthy young men? A left-right comparison of the fibre number in whole anterior tibialis muscles. Eur J Appl Physiol Occup Physiol 1991, 62:301-304.

66.   Tamaki T, Akatsuka A, Tokunaga M, Ishige K, Uchiyama S, Shiraishi T: Morphological and biochemical evidence of muscle hyperplasia following weight-lifting exercise in rats. Am J Physiol 1997, 273:C246-256.

67.   McCall GE, Byrnes WC, Dickinson A, Pattany PM, Fleck SJ: Muscle fiber hypertrophy, hyperplasia, and capillary density in college men after resistance training. J Appl Physiol (1985) 1996, 81:2004-2012.

About the Author

John Thacker Jr. was born to a Coast Guard family, and spent his early years moving from coast to coast every few years. The experience exposed him to many different people and cultures, and allowed him to develop the ability to adapt quickly to change. In college, John wrestled for his school, after which he never really stopped going to the gym. John developed this program while earning his MBA from the University of Louisville, and continues to use the Nephilim Barbell Program to this day. The Nephilim Barbell Program is designed for busy professionals, and John fits the mold, having earned his black belt in Lean Six Sigma and using it to transform the logistics industry. John lives in beautiful Edina Minnesota with his trophy wife and two kids (one boy and one girl), and enjoys living a balanced and full life that includes moving heavy objects around for fun.

The author with one of his heavy toys